# How Universities Work

# How Universities Work

John V. Lombardi

Johns Hopkins University Press • Baltimore

© 2013 Johns Hopkins University Press
All rights reserved. Published 2013
Printed in the United States of America on acid-free paper
9 8 7 6 5 4 3 2 1

Johns Hopkins University Press
2715 North Charles Street
Baltimore, Maryland 21218-4363
www.press.jhu.edu

Library of Congress Cataloging-in-Publication Data

Lombardi, John V.
    How universities work / John V. Lombardi.
        pages cm
    Includes bibliographical references and index.
    ISBN 978-1-4214-1122-4 (pbk.) — ISBN 978-1-4214-1123-1 (electronic)—
ISBN 1-4214-1122-9 (pbk.) — ISBN 1-4214-1123-7 (electronic)    1. Education,
Higher—United States.    2. Education, Higher—United States—Administration.
3. Universities and colleges—United States.    4. Universities and colleges—
United States—Administration.    I. Title.
    LA227.4.L65 2013
    378—dc23

                        2013010162

A catalog record for this book is available from the British Library.

*Special discounts are available for bulk purchases of this book. For more information,
please contact Special Sales at 410-516-6936 or specialsales@press.jhu.edu.*

Johns Hopkins University Press uses environmentally friendly book materials,
including recycled text paper that is composed of at least 30 percent post-
consumer waste, whenever possible.

*For*
*Molly, Alexandra, and Samantha*

# Contents

# Preface

This little book introduces the world of university management. Many people become involved with the management of higher education institutions. While they may have extensive experience with other complex organizations as well as having been college students, they may not have an adequate frame of reference for understanding the processes that make universities successful. Trustees, faculty, students, legislators, alumni, newly appointed department chairs and deans, and even some experienced administrators may find this book useful.

*How Universities Work* emphasizes research universities, institutions that participate significantly in the intensely competitive world of academic research. Although they form a relatively small percentage of the total number of postsecondary institutions and enroll a modest fraction of the total U.S. student population, they also represent many of the most prestigious universities. Their faculty and staff help define the nation's research agenda, and their approach to undergraduate, graduate, and postgraduate education tends to set a standard followed in varying degrees by the rest of the higher education industry. Most of the faculty and administration who have doctoral degrees acquire their academic values through their graduate experience at research universities.

American research universities compete in and perhaps dominate the global university marketplace. As more countries join this competition, the techniques and operation of successful research institutions become ever more important. Most nations recognize that global economic prosperity requires a major investment in the development and operation of a dynamic university sector in their countries. They believe that successful performance by their national research universities signals a nation capable of participating at the highest levels in global economic competition. This academic competitive achievement leads, many believe, to a stronger national presence in all areas of international activity and serves as a symbol of power and significance among the community of nations. Reflecting these beliefs, international efforts to measure the preeminence of national research programs have gained increasing attention, and technical arguments about the best methods for measuring research productivity and quality are highly sophisticated and fierce.

*How Universities Work* does not resolve these global issues, but its approach reflects the larger conversation and focuses on effective ways to drive U.S. institutions to succeed within this context. This is not a cookbook for university administrators but a pragmatic approach to understanding the structure and dynamics of these remarkable institutions. Many will, of course, disagree with opinions and perspectives included here, but that is all to the good, as this book is the result of constant discussion. Further commentary will improve our understanding.

Throughout the United States, universities of all types struggle to understand and adjust to competition, variable public support, resistance to tuition, dissatisfaction with various aspects of university life, endless demands for accountability, financial constraints, and a wide range of technological, bureaucratic, and organizational challenges. At the same time, universities find themselves ever more essential to the attainment of what most Americans consider a good life. Study after study demonstrates that a college education is a recognized prerequisite for access to middle-class standing in America.

Parents seek educational advantages for their children at the earliest opportunity, and competition for places at prestigious institutions at every level of education, from preschool to graduate and professional programs, remains intense. Some states in the South, Southwest, and West struggle to meet a growing demand for access from expanding populations. Others adjust to stable or even declining numbers of traditional college-aged students. The nation expects the continued production of university research to drive global economic competitiveness, and each region and state looks to its universities to support the local economic development that promotes prosperity and promises higher-paying jobs for its residents.

In this context, the management of universities, always more of an art than a science, challenges creativity and commitment. Faculty guilds seek higher pay, greater security, and more autonomy. Student clients and customers demand higher quality, lower cost, greater attention to their expectations, and more extensive amenities. Supporters in legislatures and the public seek better education for lower cost and with a higher yield. Alumni and donors expect high achievement and nationally distinguished programs in all areas, including winning sports teams.

These expectations produce countervailing pressures on the institutions, their people, and their management tools. Universities must become more effective and efficient even as their traditional sources of funds contract. They must become more conscious of quality even as the pressure for lower costs grows stronger. They must seek greater support even as the public asks for better proof of their value. The highly selective, research-oriented institutions must compete with each other for scarce talented and high-quality faculty and students and for the money that supports the programs these talented people expect.

Institutions meet these challenges in different ways. Some universities disappear behind a facade of complex and confusing discussions about institutional management, expecting the public to tire of the constant confusion of purpose that often characterizes university rhetoric. They hope that the public clamor for reform will pass. Many academic administrators develop this technique to a fine art. They create complex measures that measure nothing or the wrong things. They divide, subdivide, and regress their programs and activities into such a proliferation of differentiated products that no external observer can measure the comparative effectiveness of their work. Above all, they articulate high-sounding goals focused on values and philosophy and participate in current enthusiasms for technological wizardry without, in most cases, offering a clear method for measuring results.

Other universities recognize the pressures for change as natural and inevitable consequences of the growing global competitiveness that has challenged all of America's great international industries. These institutions know that academics must confront these changes and respond to them directly and clearly; otherwise, sooner or later their universities will stagnate and decline.

*How Universities Work* focuses on meeting the challenge of competitiveness with an emphasis on the public and private research university. It explores a variety of subjects related to the effective operation of universities on the premise that good management is essential. It starts from the recognition that competitive universities of any type must provide high quality and high productivity because successful institutions drive both quality and productivity. Universities in search of improvement must measure their quality and productivity, and this book focuses on the organizational and structural characteristics of universities with a special emphasis on their impact on management and improvement.

This book follows the money. Universities articulate their values most clearly as they manage revenue and expenses. When universities follow the money, they must measure quality and productivity to invest in improved performance. These topics serve less to offer a single optimal strategy and more to develop the tools for analysis and action. Universities have different histories and are located in widely different economic, political, and organizational spaces. Every university, however, must confront the same issues and problems, and the tools discussed here serve the interests of every kind of institution.

# Acknowledgments

University life offers a remarkable opportunity to work with people of widely varying skills, abilities, and interests. Over the years, colleagues at Indiana University's campuses, the Johns Hopkins University, the University of Florida, the University of Massachusetts Amherst, and the Louisiana State University system campuses offered examples, inspiration, and guidance in understanding universities. Librarians and businesspeople, activists and politicians, donors and sports fans, alumni and trustees, and especially the students, faculty, and staff of these institutions shared insight and perspective. Like life itself, university experiences range from the inspirational to the disappointing, but the energy, dynamism, and commitment of most of those who engage with these institutions bear testimony to the fundamental strength of these places.

This book on how universities work began with a series of graduate courses initiated at the University of Florida with Betty Phillips (formerly Capaldi) and continued in Massachusetts and Louisiana. It also owes much to the work of the Center for Measuring University Performance (MUP Center), created with the exceptional support of Lewis Schott, a generous alumnus of the University of Florida. Over the last decade or so, the MUP Center's staff, advisors, and commentators have addressed a wide range of significant issues related to university competition, performance, and improvement. With the collaborative leadership of Betty Phillips, the MUP Center has remained actively involved in the international conversation about university issues and challenges. This book has benefited not only from the research of MUP Center colleagues but also from the close reading and comments provided by its staff of Craig Abbey, Diane Craig, and Lynne Collis, along with the careful assistance of its current advisory board of Lloyd Armstrong, Art Cohen, Larry Goldstein, Gerardo Gonzalez, Roger Kaufman, and Richard Stanley. Especially in chapter 1, but throughout this book, the impact of the MUP Center's work and publications is clearly evident.

John Armstrong, Paul Doherty, Gene Isenberg, and Gordon Oakes, friends of the University of Massachusetts Amherst, offered support, advice, and insight, and they stand in the place of those trustees, volunteers, and donors whose engagement with colleges and universities transcends any personal or political commitments. Over the years, at various institutions, the quality of many trustees, volunteers, and donors, who dedicate time, intellect, and fortune to the improvement of their institutions, serves to motivate their university colleagues to higher levels of performance.

A special place in these acknowledgments belongs to John W. Ryan (1929–2011), whose friendship, wisdom, and support from 1967 to 2011 made so many things possible and whose academic leadership at Indiana University, the State University of New York, and other institutional and international venues set such a high standard of academic stewardship.

Over almost a half century, Germán Carrera Damas, distinguished Venezuelan historian and academic, has shared his wide-ranging international perspective and deep understanding of academic and intellectual affairs in countless conversations reflected in many ways through this book.

An extended family of university presidents and chancellors helped with understanding the sometimes mysterious ways of university life. Among those, Gordon Gee, president of the Ohio State University, continues to set his mark on higher education leadership and helped with this project; Steve Trachtenberg, president emeritus of the George Washington University, encouraged the completion of this book; and Michael Crow, president of Arizona State University, offered his support. Kathy Waldron, president of William Paterson University, and John Schwaller, president of SUNY Potsdam, shared their experiences since our time together at Indiana University. William Bulger, during his term as president of the University of Massachusetts System, provided significant insight on many issues.

In addition to the colleagues mentioned above, this book benefited from the advice and careful commentary of Charlena Seymour (Simmons College), Paul Kostecki (UMass Amherst), Ray Lamonica (LSU), Wendy Simoneaux (LSU system), Mike Gargano (University of Texas Health Science Center at San Antonio), and Joe Corso (LSU system). A long friendship with Paul Robell (University of Florida) provided invaluable perspectives on higher education fund raising and alumni support for this and other projects, and John Lordan (Fordham University) has shared his expertise ever since we worked together at Johns Hopkins University. Carolyn Roberts, an exceptional trustee and regent and long-time leader within the Florida higher education community, offered her always generous support to this project among so many others.

In recent years, *Inside Higher Ed* has been a source of information and commentary essential to all of us in colleges and universities. It has been a pleasure to participate in its work through a blog ("Reality Check") and other occasional contributions, thanks to the encouragement and engagement of its editor, Doug Lederman, and his colleagues. Many of the *Inside Higher Ed* items have their echoes in this book.

At the University of Massachusetts Amherst, the current chancellor, Kumble Subbaswamy, offered significant support during the final preparation of this work, along with that university's librarian Jay Schafer. The editorial board and staff of Johns Hopkins University Press, and especially its editor-in-chief, Greg Britton, demonstrated generosity and expertise in bringing this work into existence. Special thanks go also to Kira Bennett for her wise editorial contributions and to Kim

Johnson, Senior Production Editor at JHU Press, for shepherding this book to completion.

M. Luciana Lombardi, musician, librarian, historian, bibliographer, indexer, and a constant participant and observer of academic and cultural institutions, provided her expert services in the preparation of the index.

For a half century of college and university life, Cathryn Lombardi has been a constant partner and participant. Her remarkable ability to capture the spirit and enthusiasm of university people created a partnership that has led us to many academic venues and created countless opportunities. Without her collaboration, the experience that this book reflects would not have happened.

Spring 2013

*How Universities Work*

*Chapter 1*

# Quality Engines

------------------------------------------------------------------

## The American Research University Prototype

Even though research universities demonstrate a bewildering variety in the details of their organization, all of them express a common institutional prototype. This prototype models the behavior of research universities as organizations, even if, like all synthetic constructs, it does not represent the operations of any particular institution in detail. The research university, like most higher education institutions, pursues multiple missions that engage teaching and service. Even the most intensely competitive and successful research universities deliver full undergraduate instructional programs. While the American research universities have many distinctive features that differentiate them from colleges and universities that emphasize teaching and service, almost all institutions share a common undergraduate structure and purpose. Nonetheless, a clear understanding of the top American research universities serves to clarify the behavior of the larger number of colleges and universities that follow their lead.

The model presented here views research universities as organizations with two related, closely linked, but operationally relatively independent structures.

- The first is an *academic core*, composed of a group of faculty guilds that have primary responsibility for the academic content and quality of the enterprise.
- The second is an *administrative shell*, responsible for the acquisition and distribution of resources and for the management of the enterprises that support the faculty guilds as well as the interaction with external governance of boards and political institutions.

## The Academic Core

Faculty guilds are the most important part of the university because they define and create the university's academic substance. The guilds enable the university's many other functions related to teaching and research. Disciplinary considerations define guilds, such as chemistry, history, physics, psychology, philosophy, medicine, and law.

Moreover, within the university, each faculty guild serves as the local branch of a national guild of the same specialty. For example, all professors in a university history department belong to the same national guild, even though the local university employs them. The national guild establishes the intellectual standards for their work; the local university deals with their employment and work assignments.

The same holds true for chemists, psychologists, and the members of other guilds. Each guild defines itself in terms of the intellectual methodology that its members apply to their field of study. Historians, for example, have a methodology for the use of historical evidence in the development of explanations about past events.

The guild's definition of standards based on these methods and the evaluation of quality based on the standards are what define the guild's responsibility. Members of the guild must meet these academic and methodological standards, or the guild will not recognize the validity of their work.

As has been the case for all guilds since medieval times, the methodological standards guarantee that the members' products meet guild criteria. If a guild-certified historian writes a biography of Simón Bolívar, for example, we can have confidence that the interpretation presented uses documents and evidence in accord with the history guild's standards of accuracy and reliability. The guild does not guarantee the correctness of the resulting interpretation, only that the guild-certified historian used appropriate methodology properly in ways that permit other expert members of the guild to review and validate that work.

The same is true in science, which perhaps offers a better illustration. Scientists have precise methodologies, both for doing their work and for reporting and validating its results. When physicists present the results of their work, most people lack the expertise to evaluate the scientific validity of the process used to arrive at the announced result. Instead, the public relies on a validation by the physics guild before accepting any result as a reliable scientific finding.

Each guild has its own process for validating the work done by its members and for reviewing results presented by aspirants for membership or advancement in the guild. All guilds, however, rely on a variation of the peer-review system that mobilizes the talents of expert guild members to assess the work of other guild members. This process often involves experts replicating the experiments and reexamining the results before presentation to the public through publication. Whatever the process, however, the guild sets and enforces the standards for the field to ensure the quality of guild-certified results.

Analytical methodology, more than subject matter studied, distinguishes one guild from another. Although historians and sociologists study similar phenomena (revolution, poverty, social change), they employ significantly different methodologies that separate the sociologists' guild from the historians' guild, and the guild products provide answers to substantially different questions.

The expanding range of knowledge constantly produces new information and suggests new explanations. These, in turn, often require new methodologies. Over time, new guilds emerge with definable methodologies that serve to advance understanding. In other cases, efforts to create new guilds do not succeed because no coherent, intellectually sound, and distinct methodology emerges.

The guild does not pass judgment primarily on whether a scholar's idea is right or wrong; rather, it ensures that scholarly ideas receive rigorous analysis and proof regardless of the political or personal interests that may surround them. Scientists may believe that they have found the key to eternal life, but public acceptance of this result requires validation by other members of the appropriate science guilds through a critical review according to applicable methodological standards.

The guilds also define the university's undergraduate curriculum in a negotiated conversation with other guilds, mediated and guided by institutional authorities. This negotiation establishes the content and delivery of knowledge contained in the traditional frame of four-year undergraduate degree programs. Each component of this degree reflects guild-certified knowledge. Doctoral and other advanced degree programs belong almost exclusively to their respective guilds.

Finally, the guild controls the acquisition, promotion, tenure, and retention of faculty. Although other actors in the university (administrators, union officials, students, and others) influence this process in various ways, the guild holds primary responsibility for the quality of the faculty. Because their own members hire and retain their successors, an institution's guilds behave as self-replicating organizations.

If the guilds replicate themselves at the same quality level, the university overall will maintain its current level of quality. If they replace themselves at a lower level, the university declines, and if they hire their replacements at a higher level of quality, the university improves. Research universities pay close attention to guild management of faculty talent because they know that a university's quality and productivity depend on the faculty.

A diagram of the core structure of the model research university would show a number of guilds, each separate from the others, linked by their common participation in the instructional enterprise and by their common concern for the support and promotion of research. They would appear as separate entities, because the members of one guild cannot generally participate in the work of another except as guests or in jointly owned interdisciplinary projects. Members of one guild may not normally transfer their academic standing directly to another guild without a complete review of their qualifications by the other guild.

The guilds of any individual university also appear as separate entities to emphasize that they belong intellectually more to their national guild than to their local university. The national guild sets the common methodological standards for determining the quality and reliability of its products. Local guilds apply these common methodological standards whether resident in a university in New York or Texas, Minnesota or California. However, the level of productivity and quality required for membership in each local guild will vary from university to university.

In major research universities, as an example, the local history guilds will require new members to possess not only a PhD, with a dissertation completed and approved according to the standards of the guild, but also a record of publication in significant peer-reviewed journals and the promise of a major scholarly book. For permanent status within these high-quality local guilds, historians will publish at least two major peer-reviewed books. At a comprehensive state university, the level of research quality and productivity expected by the local history guild for permanent status will include perhaps only the completion of a PhD and the publication of one or two peer-reviewed articles. The standards are the same, but the level of performance can differ.

A university's quality and competitiveness depend on the quality and competitiveness of its faculty, and the local guild sets the level of performance for new and continuing faculty members. The university's academic standing, then, is the aggregate result of the success of each of these local guilds in the recruitment and retention of faculty. This model of guild behavior applies to competitive research universities and sets standards recognized generally by most other colleges and universities.

*This guild stuff sounds positively medieval,* says the chemistry graduate student taking a course on university management. *Aren't we in a modern, technological age?* The professor answers, *Think of silversmiths. If you buy a silver teapot, you don't want the handle to fall off when you pour the tea, so you look for the silversmiths' mark that tells you the guild guarantees the quality of your teapot. The same holds for chemistry.* Looking at the professor as if he might have insulted chemists, the student says, *What do you mean?* The professor reassures her, *I know nothing about chemistry, but I want to be sure that the chemistry taught to my children is correct and that the chemistry research that underlies my medicine was done right. If the chemistry guild certifies these products, I have confidence.* *OK,* the student says, happy that the professor has admitted his chemical ignorance, *but if I'm a silversmith, why can't I go work as a cabinetmaker?* The professor says, *You can, but you have to start at the bottom as an apprentice and meet the cabinetmaker guild standards, since the skills of a silversmith are different than those of a cabinetmaker. But,* the professor adds, *you can go work as a master silversmith immediately in any town that has a branch of the silversmiths' guild.*

## The Administrative Shell

The second structure within the American research university is the administrative shell that surrounds and supports the guilds. Most observers see the shell when they first encounter the university. The shell contains a traditional business structure, hierarchical and orderly, with a chain of command as well as the other accoutrements of modern corporate America. It provides the formal, legal governance mechanism of the university, including a board of trustees or regents. It identifies a president, vice presidents, deans, other administrators, and members of faculty senates who carry out corporate line and staff functions on behalf of the university and manage governance as well as administrative issues.

To most people, this is the university's management. In one sense, this is true. The board has fiduciary responsibility and usually is the final source of authority for the university. The president is legally responsible for the institution's management. The vice presidents and deans report through an administrative hierarchy. The faculty senate approves new degrees and curricular changes.

At the same time, the people in the shell do not actually do the work that makes the university valuable. That work takes place primarily in the guilds or under guild supervision. The shell mobilizes and distributes resources that support the work of the guilds, and it protects the guilds from harmful external forces. The shell manages the interactions among guilds. Most importantly, the shell manages the university's money and creates the incentives that motivate guild behavior.

Participants in the administrative shell typically demonstrate a fondness for public displays of institutional homogeneity, as expressed in the form of mission statements, strategic plans, and the like. These high-minded products generally have minor impact on the guilds and their work—unless the shell administrators match these plans with the incentives created by the distribution of money. The criteria for distributing money create much stronger incentives for guild behavior than do strategic plans and mission statements articulated by institutional leaders for inspirational purposes.

Deans and department chairs occupy a special intermediate role between the functions of the shell and those of the core guilds. While deans, and chairs to a somewhat lesser extent, serve as administrative officers in the formal organization of the university, they serve more as guild representatives to the shell than as administrative managers of the core.

Deans receive their appointments from vice presidents and presidents, and they recognize their responsibility to these shell officers. Deans also know that their success depends on their ability to earn and retain the respect and support of their fellow guild members and to represent guild interests successfully in the competition for resources managed by the shell organization.

Department and program chairs respond even more closely to the interests of their guild colleagues than do deans. We might think of deans and chairs as guild masters, for they manage the operation of the guilds both on behalf of the guild members and on behalf of the shell organization.

In this model, it is important to focus on institutional purpose. Some might say that the research university produces students, research products, economic development, and public service. While the university does produce these things, the delivery of goods and services to society is actually a secondary, even if significant, benefit from the university's primary pursuit of internal quality as represented by research and students.

## Quality Engines

Research universities exist to accumulate the highest level and the greatest amount of internal academic quality possible. The goal is to gather inside the university the most research-productive faculty, the brightest students, and the highest-quality academic and cultural environment achievable.

Although the research university delivers a wide variety of products to external constituencies, such as graduates, technology, economic development, and public service, its primary focus is on the creation of internal quality. This is why we call research universities "quality engines."

In pursuing the goal of maximum internal quality, the research university will almost automatically graduate its students, promote economic development, and serve the public interest. However, the production of these goods and services does not drive university success, although it may motivate others to help the institution succeed.

The model clearly illustrates a relationship between the academic core of guilds and the university's shell. The shell's primary responsibility is to find the money necessary to compete for the best faculty (including all of the subsidies for their research) and for the best students (including all of the amenities and academic and educational enhancements that attract them).

The shell organizes structures and systems to raise private endowments and gifts, to lobby for public funds, to compete for federal dollars, to seek foundation revenue, and to create a hospitable and supportive academic and cultural environment. The shell raises this money and creates this environment so the guilds will succeed in recruiting and retaining quality faculty, in subsidizing research, and in promoting similar activities that create internal quality.

Shell participants often take a more direct role in the recruitment and retention of undergraduate students, in whom the guild has less of a direct interest. The interactions between the guilds and the shell, and between the shell and the external environment, are much more complex and more closely interrelated than presented here. Nonetheless, the model of quality engines focuses our attention on the research university's revenue-seeking behavior in support of the guild's success and by extension the institution's success in the competition for quality.

The model sees the university as an enterprise that is its own primary customer. On the surface, this appears contradictory, since the revenue that supports the university comes from outside the institution and the institution relentlessly organizes itself to capture as much revenue from all of these sources as possible.

Most observers would assume that the university sells a product or service directly to those who provide it with money. While the university does provide value to those who pay, the process that it uses to provide the value and the mechanisms for payment dilute much of the relationship between buyer and seller that characterizes transactions in the commercial world.

Research universities market the talent of their research faculty and staff to the federal government, private foundations, and corporations in exchange for funding to do research. At the same time, universities invest their own funds from other sources to subsidize research facilities and talent to gain a competitive advantage in competition for grants.

The universities compete against each other for federal grants, but they also invest their internal funds heavily for the opportunity to compete. The funds that universities use to subsidize the competition for federal research come from annual giving, earnings on endowment, state agencies, returns on patents and licenses, internal savings, and other surplus-generating activities.

Instead of seeing the university as a producer of goods and services for an external competitive marketplace, we can think of the university as a consumer of the quality that it purchases from the external marketplace. In this view, the university maximizes its revenue from all sources to purchase quality research, students, faculty, and academic environment. It then uses the existence of this quality environment to attract additional external investors who buy access to the environment and contribute to its creation rather than purchasing ownership of any particular university product.

*Wait, wait,* says the impatient business executive trustee to the professor. *Universities exist to produce students and research and service for the public just like I make appliances for the public. This quality engine stuff doesn't make sense.* The professor, with the infinite patience of the true teacher, says, *No, we produce quality. The students come to get it, the businesses come to use it, and the economy comes to take advantage of it, but we produce it for its own sake. Not so,* says the executive. *I buy the services of the university for my children as students.* The professor says, *Not exactly. Think of Disney World. You buy admission to take advantage of the quality inside, but you take away the experience, and your experience may be different than mine. You go to Disney World because you think it has accumulated the highest-quality attractions of any amusement park in the world. Like Disney World, the university has more quality than anyone can experience, and each person chooses those parts of the university quality they want to engage, just as you and your children choose different attractions.* The business exec isn't happy with this comparison and says, *Maybe, but universities are really different.* The professor says, *Sure, but the key issue is that the value of Disney World, compared to other similar parks, is that it has more quality inside its boundaries than others do. Our university wants to do the same: have more quality inside. Then you and everyone else will want to come to take advantage of the quality. Absent the quality, you won't come.* The executive says, *Hmmm, let me think about that.*

The goal of research universities, then, is to accumulate the highest level and the largest amount of quality they can through the competitive purchase of scarce quality elements. Whether the institution is an elite private institution with a $14-billion endowment and $266 million of federally funded research or a public institution just barely over the $40-million level of federal research with an endowment of only $15 million, they behave in remarkably similar ways.

The details of the revenue-seeking behavior of individual universities vary depending on circumstances, history, opportunities, and whether they are under private or public control. The performance of all research universities, however, depends on success in the pursuit of the maximum accumulation of research and undergraduate student quality.

## Chapter 2

# Management

---

This book is about managing universities with a special emphasis on research universities. Management is a technique, not an end in itself. Academics use a collection of tools and processes as they implement the values and achieve the objectives of their institutions.

Universities are not random collections of people operating without system or organization, and like all organizations, they must have management. Institutional managers have many options. They can do things on the spur of the moment or manage through rigid inflexible hierarchies. They can respond to external pressures or internal politics. They can manage by objective or manage with zero-based budgeting. They can do value-based management. They can follow systems of *Total Quality Management* or *Continuous Quality Improvement*. They can implement participatory or autocratic, bottom-up or top-down management.

Whatever the name, all universities do management. The more complicated the academic enterprise the more management it requires. While many observers of higher education complain about administration (another word for management), everyone wants the right classes offered at the right time and in the right sequence, their bills paid, federal and state regulations adhered to, student health and welfare watched, safety assured, and buildings and grounds maintained. Management or administration does all of this and much more.

Often the university needs people with specific skills to manage safety, deal with plant and construction, recruit and retain students, operate athletic programs, and perform other specialized tasks. When these tasks are done well, the university runs smoothly, but when they are performed poorly, the university—its students, faculty, and staff—are left to struggle with endless problems that divert time and effort from the main business of effective teaching and research. There is a balance in university operations between too much and not enough administration, and part of the art of managing universities is to manage with minimal expense and maximal effect.

## Management Themes

Management is essential to the success of any organization, and many experts give advice. Bookstores carry shelves of how-to books on management theory and practice. They offer different sequences of magic steps guaranteed to produce business success, often coining a catchy phrase to capture the essential meaning of their management prescriptions. Frequently, these books reflect the achievements of particular businesspeople who attribute their success to the special principles outlined in their book (and by inference to the brilliance and wisdom of the authors). They tend to downplay the accidental nature of much business success. Living in boom times makes many heroes; struggling through a recession produces multiple business failures.

If read carefully—and everyone should read some of them— most management books focus on the obvious. They identify some simple principles and present them in effective ways. The core principles are:

- Know the business.
- Know the customers.
- Appreciate the employees.
- Compete against the market.
- Pay attention to the money.

Everything else elaborates on these themes. Much of what appears in management books is stylistic rather than substantive. Some talk about managing by walking around or managing by example. All of this is style that reflects primarily methods of communication. While style is surely interesting and useful, it does not replace the substance of management.

Popular books on management usually charm the reader with a skillful, breezy style, but often they make no allowance for the complexities of organizations and the widely varying characteristics and circumstances of different enterprises. Everything that a management guru says works somewhere, in some business, under some circumstances.

Many such books have interesting insights, but most offer buzzwords that often fail to clarify the specific challenges of real organizations. Indeed, if a science of management existed, we would need only a few books to explain it. The proliferation of *how-to-succeed-in-management* books reassures us that management is a practical art performed in real time, not an experimental science with specific, definable results. Indeed, the *Dilbert* comic strip frequently highlights the accidental nature of business success or failure.

Those who observe and study academic management in similar organizations over time discover that managers (deans, department chairs, program directors, vice presidents or chancellors, and provosts, for example) employ highly diverse styles and techniques and nonetheless achieve great success. Others with identical styles using similar techniques achieve much less.

Style and technique are not the core issues of management. They have their purposes and uses, but they do not replace the substance of management, nor do they replace the essential component of fortunate circumstances or plain, simple good luck.

## Management Principles

We too have our core principles that define successful academic management:

- Money matters.
- Performance counts.
- Time is the enemy.

*Money matters* because every academic institution requires money to survive and prosper. It is possible to have much money and still perform badly, but it is not possible to be a poor institution and compete in the marketplace against much better-funded universities. Money determines the range and depth of activities and defines how much an institution can spend on generating quality in addition to doing the basic work of teaching. As is true for every other enterprise, public or private, for-profit or nonprofit, money allows the institution to fulfill its mission.

*A university is not a business,* they say. I ask, *Have you ever been to a church? Do you remember how it goes? The preacher preaches, and the faithful respond. The organ plays, and the congregation sings. Those fallen from grace find their faith, and the penitent are saved. Then comes the offering. The music swells with uplifting cadences, the preacher calls out for a higher power to inspire the congregation, and the deacons pass the plate. The experienced minister, recognizing the unsatisfactory sound of clinking coins, calls out for the crinkle of paper, the sounds of a generous spirit. He reminds us that faith alone cannot perform good works, which require tangible support from the faithful, that the roof leaks, and that the heating system will not make it through the winter. The organist pulls out all the stops, the deacons pass through the congregation once again, and the offering transitions from coin to paper. At the end, the preacher thanks the divine inspiration that prompted such generosity, making another week of God's work possible. We in the university, I say, also pursue higher truths, and our institutions, like any small rural church, know that academic inspiration also requires tangible revenue from the faithful.*

In research universities, money is particularly important because research is essentially a money-losing proposition. Even when we have a large grant to do some project, the grant almost never covers the full cost of the project. The university will have to subsidize some portion of the true costs. The more money we can generate that is not required for some other purpose, the more research grants we can acquire and the more competitive our institution will be.

While tuition and fees, plus state support for public institutions, may cover basic instruction, high-quality academic and extracurricular student experiences usually require extra funding. If the university has extra money (what we call marginal dollars), it can spend it on smaller classes, honors programs, special teaching materials, equipment or facilities, student life activities, and many other amenities that make student life attractive, including intercollegiate sports.

Money matters, and the more money a university has above what it costs to operate the core teaching mission, the more competitive it will be in the marketplace.

*Performance counts* because the competition among colleges and universities is driven by the work of the best students and faculty. High-performing institutions whose students and faculty work at the top level in their fields are also the most prestigious and the most successful in continuing to attract the best students and faculty. Performance counts as well because when every element of the institution operates at top levels of effectiveness, the institution will achieve much more with the money available than if the performance of its people is subpar.

This means the physical plant staff and the admission officers, the fund-raising professionals, and the student services staff must all perform at the top levels characteristic of others in their fields. Faculty must teach, research, publish, and seek grants at levels of performance that at least meet their competition.

Performance is contagious. When the university concentrates on measurable competitive performance, everyone tends to participate. If the faculty perform at top levels, so too will the students. If the campus maintains buildings and grounds at top levels, admissions and retention officers will find it easier to compete for the best students.

I looked out the window. The quad, designed by famous architects to present an elegant, wide lawn that formed an entryway to the campus, was filled with dandelions. The grass, although recently cut, spilled over the curbs all around. *Why can't we get rid of the dandelions?* I asked. *Why can't we trim the edges so the place looks like we care? Oh,* they said, *it's expensive.* Taking executive prerogative for a rant, I responded, *More expensive than losing prospective students whose parents think a place that can't trim the edges or remove the weeds is unlikely to have serious faculty and good staff? Who chooses a restaurant with trash on the outside? Our visitors can't see what goes on in the chemistry lab, but they can sure see that we can't fix the lawn.* The dandelions disappeared, the edges got trimmed, and people (faculty, staff, students, visitors, alumni) said, *Wow, the campus looks great. Things must be looking up!* If you don't care about the place, who will believe you care about the people?

Performance is the reference point for the marketplace, and what we measure when we identify a high-quality university is the quality performance of its people.

*Time is the enemy* because every minute university people do not use to apply for a grant, recruit a student, repair a classroom, or do some other critical job, competitor institutions are applying for the grant, recruiting the student, or repairing their classrooms. Universities live in an intense marketplace, and time is the enemy because university organization can permit complacency and delay.

Public and private research universities are among the world's most enduring institutions. They are rarely at risk of elimination or total failure. University people often have a false sense of stability, believing that this longevity is also a guarantee of future performance. It is not.

Every university wants to have what better universities have. The only way to get what some other institution has is to compete for it. We want better students, but everyone wants better students, and the number of better students is limited. If we fail to recruit a good student today, some other institution will, and our moment to win is lost.

If we do not apply for a grant today, someone else will get the grant, and the moment to win is lost. If we do not visit our alumni and friends and ask for a gift today, the moment to gain support for our ambitions is lost. Time is the enemy.

*We've got to fix the problem,* I said. *OK,* the experts responded. *Here are five things we might do, but we'll need to get everyone to buy in. We'll develop a proposal, schedule several meetings over the next few months, present the recommendations, and discuss them. By the end of the semester, we'll have some solutions to begin implementing.* I said, *Let's send out the five things in an e-mail to the entire faculty, staff, and student body explaining the problem and the possible solutions. We'll give everyone a week to respond with revisions or improvements.* They said, *That's pretty fast.* I said, *E-mail is pretty fast.* So on Monday we sent out the five things. Four days later, we had several hundred responses from all parts of the campus with 20 percent good ideas. We incorporated the 20 percent good ideas, reissued the revised five things the next Monday, and announced another window for comment that closed the following Wednesday. By Wednesday at five in the afternoon, we had thirty responses: half from people who didn't want any change and half with useful suggestions. On Friday we implemented the revised and improved five solutions, and the problem went away. Two weeks, start to finish. Time is the enemy.

Effective competition requires us to understand something about the university world, its development, and its functions. Research universities are a small part of the higher education industry, and their importance within this industry has changed significantly over the years.

Many have written thoughtfully (and some not so thoughtfully) about the purpose and values of a university and a university education. Although the history of higher education is a complex subject, our interest here is somewhat less grand.

## The American Research University

We focus on the American university and, within that context, on the current incarnation of a particular type of institution, the American research university. The evolution of the American university since its earliest days in both public and private forms set the patterns that even today, many generations later, govern how we think about institutions of higher education.

In America, even more than in other parts of the world, the college or university has always had a utilitarian, pragmatic value at its core. While the purpose of education as a provider of enlightenment and wisdom is surely embedded in the structure and content of colleges and universities, from the beginning American universities served to train men and, later, women for specific functional and productive roles in society.

Whether by training ministers or farmers, engineers or doctors, teachers or scientists, the American college and university justified its existence primarily on its ability to deliver value to individuals and meet society's needs for experts. Whether focusing on preaching, mining, or business, these institutions expected their graduates to take leadership roles and add value to society.

At the beginning, the college and university had an elitist cast, serving to replicate the existing elite and fulfill elite roles. However, with the emergence of large public university enterprises, especially the emergence of the public land-grant institutions in the second half of the nineteenth century and their subsequent expansion during the post–World War II era, the American higher education industry became more utilitarian and more focused on ordinary people.

The land-grant institution grafted an emphasis on practical knowledge for agriculture and engineering onto the standard college curriculum designed to produce leaders well versed in the cultural and political traditions of America and Western Europe. This notion found resonance with the dramatically expanding American economy in the late nineteenth and early twentieth centuries. With the post-WWII boom in enrollment, American higher education became an essential industry for the creation of a prosperous middle class and the sustained replication of the elite leaders of business, industry, government, and the arts. America's higher education enterprise also became engaged as an active partner as the United States assumed ever-greater responsibility and asserted ever-greater authority in international affairs.

In the second half of the twentieth century and into the twenty-first, the American higher education industry grew increasingly complex, with subcategories of institutions pursuing substantially different missions, using distinct curricula, faculty, and students. This complexity resulted in some confusion among observers of higher education as they attempted to sort out what a college education might mean and how anyone could determine which one among the many thousands of higher education providers offered the best value.

We will explore many of these themes throughout this conversation about research universities, for of course the research university is a special case. Nonetheless, when we look across the higher education domain that includes community colleges, private for-profit colleges, state and regional comprehensive institutions, private liberal arts colleges, sectarian colleges, and state-sponsored and private research universities, we find that all share elements of the same set of educational values.

Their missions overlap, as does the rhetoric for describing their value. While no one would confuse a small community college in New England with a major private research university in California, the overlap in declared values and purpose is remarkable. This naturally leads to considerable confusion as we attempt to analyze performance and evaluate the roles of these colleges and universities.

Among the conflicting notions that our society holds about colleges and universities, these two highlight the significant challenges of managing universities:

- We imagine the university as a charmed place of pure thought and free inquiry, driven by the pursuit of truth and nurtured by the open exchange of conflicting ideas.
- We expect the university to be an efficient generator and transmitter of the useful knowledge that creates the American economic dream of a good life for individuals and international leadership for the nation.

The conversation about these two notions constitutes a fundamental value conflict that has engaged and will continue to engage managers of American higher education. If academics want to *know the business* and *know the customers*, they must come to some understanding of these conflicting traditions in

American higher education and reconcile them for themselves and their institutions.

In practice, colleges and universities have generally pursued both of these conflicting notions at the same time. They articulate and often deliver a context capable of encouraging free inquiry and the exchange of widely differing opinions, but they also construct educational programs, extracurricular activities, collaborations with business and industry, overseas study, and civic engagements that serve to provide students with practical, pragmatic experience useful for their pursuit of the American economic dream. Institutions strike different balances between these somewhat divergent perspectives, some emphasizing the practical and pragmatic while others focus on the academic pursuit of knowledge for its own sake.

*Chapter 3*

# Critics

------------------------------------------------------------

While Americans love their universities, they also love to criticize them. Parents and citizens see the university or college as a provider of culture and values, and they worry that these institutions may not provide the right values and culture to their students. The public worries that universities cost too much, operate inefficiently, or fail to provide adequate intellectual or practical content.

Most observers are long on complaint and short on viable solutions. The complexity and variety of universities offer multiple opportunities for critical displeasure. Something somewhere will incite the ire of this or that observer. While it is easy to reject the critics as irresponsible, as many are, it is not so easy to reject some of the fundamental themes of the critical literature. Universities do have to pay attention to cost and accountability. Institutions do have to understand the content of their curricula, and they must recognize the dangers of seeking benefit from commercial and industrial marketplaces. They do need to participate in emerging technological advances and evaluate possible reorganizations of their business models.

Long-time participants in American higher education often find the literature of complaint unpersuasive. Each generation expects colleges and universities to provide the perfect education to prepare its children for economic prosperity and leadership achievement. This unrealistic expectation that universities and colleges should be all things to all people provokes a constant critique that fails to recognize the value of the widely diverse nature of American higher education. Although some institution will offer any educational initiative that anyone wants, no place does everything for everyone.

However, in our eagerness to please our many constituencies, we often promise more than we actually deliver. Few, if any, universities or colleges can or should guarantee that everyone who enters will graduate or that everyone who graduates will find a satisfying and rewarding job. No universities or colleges can provide every skill that anyone would need to be successful in the world, and the attempt to do too much often leaves institutions without a high-quality focus.

## Critical Topics

At different times, critics focus on different themes, often reflecting national issues of the day. When America found itself in the middle of a crisis about its values during the late 1960s and early 1970s, universities found themselves caught in what we called a culture war.

Some thought the university a center of radical ideology, determined to erode fundamental American values. Others thought the university was a bastion of conservative oppression by corporations or the government. We argued about the inclusion or exclusion of voices expressing different values. We struggled over what texts should be required reading for all students. We fought over the inclusion of minority and third-world authors and of countercultural themes. We engaged with the courts on policies of affirmative action.

In an atmosphere enhanced by the bitterly controversial Vietnam War, universities became battlegrounds for issues of cultural inclusion and exclusion, of ethnic and gender diversity, and of equity. Although some of the heat has faded from these issues, many of the old battles remain unresolved in American higher education, feeding from time to time a critical attack. Are universities too expensive for all potential participants? Do they exclude or give unmerited advantage to individuals by considering race, class, ethnicity, or gender?

Other critiques turn on more operational issues. To some extent an outgrowth of the battle for accessibility to universities and colleges for people of all types and backgrounds, the university and college became caught between two conflicting notions.

On one side, faculty and students wanted to see everyone gain access for an opportunity to achieve the higher education experience that defines the good life in the minds of many. On the other side, outside observers wanted to see universities become ever more efficient and graduate all those who entered.

The challenge posed by the many public school systems in America that find it difficult to produce college-ready graduates complicates this conflict. Nonelite universities and colleges admit many students whose chances of success, given their previous preparation, are low. The university that gives these high-risk students an opportunity then encounters criticism because not enough of the high-risk students succeed.

The critics place the blame for student failure on the institution and its instructors, believing that it is the institution's responsibility to ensure success no matter what the inclination, aptitude, or preparation of the student. This critique of course confuses a process of education that requires as much commitment and preparation from the student as it does from the teacher. The symbol for this notion that all students who enter college should succeed is the much-misused graduation rate statistic.

This simple-minded statistic has its base, as do many higher education values, in the elite liberal arts college. In such a college, all students admitted are highly motivated and well prepared. Most come from stable economic and social backgrounds, and the elite college lavishes individual attention on its students.

These elite liberal arts colleges will graduate over 80 to 90 percent of the students who begin there. The residential campus, the close supervision, the small classes, the excellent faculty, the superb facilities, and the well-prepared students all support this result.

Most other institutions cannot reach this goal, and it is a goal only relevant to four-year, residential, full-time student campuses. Nonetheless, legislators and critics cry out for reforms that will ensure that the graduation rates of all colleges will rise towards this ideal goal. The goal, of course, is not reachable, and the statistic is unreliable for almost all but the most elite institutions.

*This is outrageous*, thunders the state senator from his seat on the legislative education committee. *In my business, we fire managers who have a failure rate of 50 to 60 percent like you people in higher education do. What kind of business would think that an average success rate around 50 percent is acceptable? Why, some of the colleges in this state only graduate 20 to 30 percent of their students! We must have standards. We must stop paying for ineffective higher education and reduce funding to colleges whose faculty fail to graduate most of the students.* The wise college president seated at the witness table thinks but does not say, *Sir, you are uninformed and foolish. We take the students the high schools graduate, and they don't graduate very many. Many of those we get are poorly prepared, barely read and write, and struggle to do the minimal level of college work. Many also come from families with no money, and the state fails to provide need-based aid for these students and instead provides merit aid to the well-off who vote. We have many programs that attempt to salvage these students, and it is a miracle that we get as many as half or a third of those who start at our campus through the system. When you put money on graduation rates, as you propose, you give us an incentive to pass everyone and deliver poor-quality graduates to meet your misplaced incentives. Stubborn failure to understand what education is all about limits the effectiveness of public policy.* What the president does say is, *Sir, we are surely as concerned as you are about the low graduation rate, and we have instituted many new programs that we're sure will bring those rates up over the next few years. We greatly appreciate your support and interest.* No one leaves the hearing room happy.

## Faculty Authority

Another challenge comes from those who see the modern college or university as abandoning its former standards and failing to produce graduates who can read, write, count, and reason. These critics want standards enforced; they decry what they believe to be the inflation of grades into meaningless reference points, and they often call for standardized tests to ensure minimal competencies.

Few engage the notion that when we must admit everyone and graduate most, it is unlikely that we will be able to maintain high standards. Further complicating these issues is the decline in the authority of the faculty.

Once regarded as the last word on quality and standards, today the faculty often find themselves encouraged by student evaluations and other pressures that focus on the appearance of student success to inflate grades and reduce the rigor of their courses. More prevalent in the humanities and social sciences than in mathematically based disciplines, this pressure to produce the appearance of good results for students is much more powerful than most of us want to admit.

Especially vulnerable are the humanists, whose evaluations may appear subjective (unlike scientists, whose mathematically based data provide a much less easily challenged reference). Many students do not accept a grade below an A with grace and charm; instead, they often argue, petition, and otherwise lobby to force faculty to raise a grade deemed lower than optimal.

In recent times, especially in public institutions, critics have fastened on the question of cost. Believing that universities should be more efficient and less expensive, they attack every element of university operations in hopes of finding the silver bullet that will kill rising costs.

While it is surely possible to reduce cost, and while some inefficiency remains in university and college operations, the scale of cost reduction possible without damaging the product is small. Many point to the dramatic reduction in the price of such things as consumer electronics and demand similar efficiencies from higher education.

This meaningless comparison fails because higher education, and especially the elite college or university, is above all else a service industry that depends on highly skilled employees. If we track the costs of other service enterprises, such as health care, accounting, or similar work, we find that higher education and these other individualized service industries have comparable cost and price curves, although higher education and health care have a double commitment to high-cost specialized professional staff and complex, expensive physical facilities.

Personal service industries using highly skilled professionals cannot readily increase the scale of their operations because the products they sell are, by definition of the marketplace and the consumers, individualized. The biggest complaint of a student at a large public university (which is seeking efficiency through scale) is that the student feels like "just a number."

Many innovations that do reduce cost also reduce quality in one form or another. By reducing the qualifications of the instructional staff (by substituting graduate assistants and adjunct faculty), colleges can reduce costs. By using Internet-enabled distance education and removing the interaction between faculty and students, colleges can reduce cost.

In the case of distance education, it takes a large-scale operation to produce education at a lower cost and equivalent quality because the infrastructure and management of distance education are nontrivial. Most success has been with large-scale operations, programs that serve populations unreachable by standard higher education institutions, or specialized programs that charge high prices. Many experiments with different platforms and modalities of distance education and e-learning demonstrate the potential of these new systems for expanding the tools of instruction, although current practice indicates considerable variation in the value of e-learning systems to differing postsecondary populations.

The challenges of cost reduction are not likely to be resolved soon, but the discussion is important and requires good data and better analysis rather than the simple wish that costs would decline. Costs can decline, but not without consequences.

## Reform or Revolution

Two major approaches dominate the criticism of colleges and universities. The first seeks to reform existing universities, making them better by improving their operation. This perspective, often pursued by those who believe the university is fundamentally sound, invokes tradition and values and attempts to adjust those to the practical realities of contemporary economic circumstances.

The second approach sees universities and many colleges as beyond repair in their current form or at least in serious crisis. In developing this approach, critics tend to see the institutional and faculty values of the traditional university as corrupt and self-serving, destructive of good moral and intellectual values, and generally debased from some ideal archetype.

Depending on the spirit of the observer, these critics seek the replacement of existing university structures with much different learning organizations or propose radical or reformist proposals that would clean house, change standards, and impose new ones.

Often critics come from a profoundly conservative perspective that seeks to create in the university an engine for the promotion of values and attitudes believed to have been current in a more glorious past and at the same time produce employment-ready graduates for the modern economy. Sometimes they come from a profoundly radical perspective that seeks to create a different future by deconstructing the university's fundamental texts and replacing its meritocratic values with more socially conscious prescriptions that ensure full participation and benefit to all.

In the literature of complaint and reform, and in the endless reports from distinguished groups identifying a crisis in some element or all of higher education in America, a key defect is often the absence of practical solutions. It is easy to find problems in as complicated and diverse an industry as American higher education, but it is much harder to find solutions that, however clever and insightful they appear on paper, will appeal to the parents and students whose choices about college determine the shape of the industry and that will satisfy the donors and public that provide substantial portions of the required revenue.

As the gaggle of parents and sometimes interested prospective students trail after the charming undergraduate conducting the campus tour, we hear these questions and comments: *Where will my student live? Is that the recreation center? Mom, look at that sports stadium! Son, these people sure keep the campus looking good. Is that the science building? It sure is big. How hard will it be to get into a sorority? Do you have a health center? Does the campus have universal free wireless Internet? What summer travel-abroad programs are there? Do students get football tickets? Will my daughter have any small classes with regular faculty? How much does parking cost? Can my son get into the honors program? Are the residence halls apartment-style? What services does the student center provide?* From these endless focus groups, we learn what our customers want, and most want many expensive non-academic services.

*Chapter 4*

# Characteristics

---------------------------------------------------------------

Higher education in America is an endlessly complex industry. It has providers of all sizes and qualities operating within many different organizational structures with distinct governance models. These institutions have diverse missions and compete in many highly differentiated markets.

An American cultural peculiarity assigns the same words to describe all these institutions. Although everyone knows the difference between a trade school, a community college, a religious sectarian institution, a private elite undergraduate college, or a major public or private research university, when Americans talk about higher education they often use the words *colleges*, *schools*, and *universities* interchangeably.

This device reflects the public confusion about the structure of American higher education, homogenizes the complexity of the academic environment, and obscures the great American achievement of a diverse and adaptable higher education industry. At the same time, however, it reflects the core belief that higher education is about "schooling"—that is, the acquisition of knowledge on a range of academic subjects that will likely have practical benefits.

The National Center for Education Statistics (NCES) 2012 *Digest of Education Statistics* provides data on the types and characteristics of postsecondary institutions, including detailed information on their students. A total of 4,706 institutions provided postsecondary education in the 2011–2012 academic year. This number disguises the wide range of institutional types. The 1,738 two-year institutions represent 37 percent of the total, while the 2,968 four-year institutions are the majority at 63 percent.

Our interest here is in the 682 public and 1,553 private not-for-profit four-year colleges and universities (some 733 institutions are private for-profit), and within these, our primary attention is on the two hundred or so institutions with substantial research commitment. These two hundred universities each spend at least $20 million a year, earned from federally funded research programs. This group historically is made up roughly of three-quarters public and one-quarter private universities. The top two hundred research institutions spend about 95 percent of the federally sponsored academic research funds distributed among 709 academic institutions.

If we focus on the top two hundred institutions in 2009, the range of federally sponsored research expenditures is wide. Excluding the Johns Hopkins University (at $1.6 billion dollars, whose total includes the $920 million Applied Physics Lab), the next highest is the University of Michigan Ann Arbor, with $636 million. The last on this list is Loyola University Chicago, with $23 million of federal research expenditures per year.

Another way to appreciate the complexity of the higher education system in America is to see the distribution of those students in the traditional under-25 college age group among the various types of institutions. Public four-year universities enroll 51 percent of the nation's full-time students under 25 years of age while their two-year counterparts enroll another 21 percent. Four-year private institutions enroll an additional 23 percent of this group, with the remaining full-time students in for-profit institutions accounting for the final 5 percent. Students attending part time enroll predominantly in public two-year institutions, at 66 percent, and public four-year institutions, at 24 percent, for a total of 91 percent of the part-time students in these two traditional sectors of institutions. Private four-year institutions enroll only about 6 percent of the part-time students. The remaining 3 percent of the part-time students appear in the private for-profit sector.

American higher education falls into various overlapping categories. Community and technical colleges have a tremendous following. They provide remediation for college-bound but underprepared high school students, a low-cost entry into the first two years of a baccalaureate degree program, and variable and adaptable vocational and technical education to large numbers of students. These colleges, located in and directly serving their communities, enjoy high public esteem and strong political support.

Most community and technical colleges operate in the public sector, although some proprietary for-profit and a number of private not-for-profit examples also exist. Many proprietary two-year institutions offer principally vocational training, but in recent years, the for-profit institutions have expanded into producing not only two-year academic programs but also proprietary four-year degrees.

Originally funded by local school districts, most public community and technical colleges have become dependent on state tax-based support and various federally sponsored programs. Almost all now also charge tuition and a variety of fees and distribute financial aid.

Community and technical colleges range in size from below a thousand students to above ten thousand. Some 12 percent are below a thousand students and about 17 percent above ten thousand, with the majority distributed in between these two extremes.

In most states, community colleges, four-year colleges, and universities compete for some of the same students and the same state dollars. Each definable sector of the American higher education industry has at least one association that represents its interests in Washington, DC, and to state legislators and that provides extensive information on its website. For the community colleges, the American Association of Community Colleges provides this service.

Liberal arts colleges deliver a relatively standardized four-year curriculum. Characterized for the most part by relatively small size (1,000 to 5,000 students), and modest to nonexistent graduate education or research activity, the institutions in this category range widely. Small, private, sectarian institutions provide religious instruction along with a liberal arts curriculum and offer an intellectually safe environment with predictable social, moral, and ethical values. Prestigious and expensive liberal arts colleges serve elite constituencies in a highly secular and competitive mode. They often create innovative and experimental intellectual, academic, and cultural environments. The sectarian and most of the prestigious liberal arts colleges exist in the private sector.

The Association of American Colleges and Universities represents this group of colleges but also includes large public and private research universities to support their commitment to the liberal arts. As a result, the focus of this organization is more on the issues of the liberal arts in all institutions than specifically on the concerns of small institutions. The National Association of Independent Colleges and Universities represents all sizes and types of private institutions, and while it includes large research universities, most of its members are smaller private colleges.

In between these institutions lies a wide range of generic public, private not-for-profit, and private for-profit, four-year institutions that serve primarily local or regional constituencies, although some for-profit colleges operate online on a national scale.

They offer liberal arts and applied undergraduate degrees in education, business, nursing, allied health, or engineering. They enroll anywhere from three thousand to fifteen thousand students or sometimes more. They may have some professionally oriented master's programs and perhaps a doctoral program or two.

They enroll students at varying price points, from relatively low costs for public to high costs for private for-profit institutions, and they usually have only modest, if any, participation in the national research enterprise. The American Association of State Colleges and Universities (AASCU) provides a trade group for about 420 public institutions in this category and expresses many of their concerns and values. AASCU includes some two-year colleges and various university systems among its membership as well.

Major public and private research universities in the United States follow a narrow range of organizational models. Although the internal details and relationships vary, the basic structures remain similar. They include small, elite, graduate and undergraduate institutions of perhaps five thousand students or even fewer and large public research universities reaching over fifty thousand students or more.

Some divide the graduate and undergraduate missions into two organizational clusters, but most operate both levels of instruction with the same faculty. They have a major commitment to research and graduate education through the PhD and postdoctoral levels. They have large contract and grant revenues, and many include large enterprises in medicine and, in land-grant universities, agriculture.

Most of the criticism of American universities focuses on elite institutions (both the small elite colleges and the elite public and private research universities), not only because of their size and prestige but also because their standards apply in greater or lesser measure to all other higher education institutions in America.

Two organizations speak for the research institutions. The Association of American Universities (AAU) self-selects, using rather arbitrary criteria, what its membership regards as the most prestigious private and public research universities in the United States and Canada and then represents these institutions and their interests in national forums. Many, but by no means all, of the nation's significant and productive research universities fall within this group's membership. Current membership is at sixty-two institutions.

In addition, the Association of Public and Land Grant Universities (APLU) (formerly the National Association of State Universities and Land Grant Colleges) serves as an umbrella organization for large, powerful public research universities as well as more modest state institutions. The public members of the AAU all belong to APLU. Many institutions pay dues to two or more organizations. APLU has 217 institutions, including 18 Historically Black Colleges and Universities (HBCU), plus the 33 American Indian land-grant colleges.

Overall representation of higher education comes from the American Council on Education (ACE), whose membership includes degree-granting institutions of all sizes, organizations, governance styles, and missions. Its membership has over 1,200 campus representatives plus another 200 from other higher education organizations. This description does not exhaustively detail the trade groups that represent university interests, but it provides a sample of some of the most significant organizations in this category.

Academics who manage universities must understand their institutions' places in the national structure of higher education and recognize the different competitive niches. Big public research universities cannot become elite liberal arts colleges, nor can liberal arts colleges offer the range of services available at large public land-grant institutions. Major private research universities cannot provide the same services to the public as public land-grant institutions.

University competition is intense, and institutions compete against similar institutions for some things and against much different institutions for others. To assume a simple model of the higher education industry obscures these distinctions and misrepresents the obstacles to and opportunities for institutional success.

## Ranking

One manifestation of the confusion surrounding our definitions of "university" is the dramatic expansion of the ranking industry. Ranking of American colleges and universities has reached epidemic proportions, and the determined effort to categorize institutions has spread overseas to encompass the world.

Ranking exists because there are so many institutions of such varied character, size, and composition that most people find it too hard to sort them into comparable categories. The highly competitive university and college business encourages each institution to sell itself as being the best, advertise its remarkable qualities, and showcase its many singular accomplishments.

The most visible enterprise to identify the commercial opportunity of academic rankings has been *U.S. News & World Report,* whose best college rankings have become a publishing phenomenon much imitated by other magazines, such as *Forbes,* the *Wall Street Journal, Barrons,* and many other publications. The ranking business, while profitable for many commercial publications, is nonetheless highly controversial, and the intense interest has made ranking an international industry.

The key issue in rankings is methodology. In most rankings, the goal has been to identify university or college characteristics assumed to be of interest to the public, often aimed at prospective students and their parents. In theory, a good ranking system would produce something akin to a *Consumer Reports* guide for consumers of higher education. However, the data to achieve this kind of ranking are elusive because the inputs and outputs of colleges are varied and of variable importance to different constituencies.

Moreover, existing statistics do not easily identify much of what a consumer might want to know about college life. As a result, the college rankings in the United States have tended to revert to primarily reputation-based survey results with some weighting related to the quality of the admitted student body, the wealth of the institution, and other identifiable statistical characteristics.

A difficulty for the commercial ranking business is that the actual quality of colleges and universities does not vary on an annual basis and the differences between similar colleges are so minor as to be mostly insignificant. To resolve this dilemma, keep the rankings fresh, and sell the magazines in which they appear, many commercial rankings improve or at least modify their methodologies from year to year, thereby changing the resulting rankings. They may also use significantly complex rankings schemes so that minor annual variations will move institutions up or down on the scale.

The extensive literature on rankings of this kind often focuses on the circular nature of the process of quantifying reputation. If a college has the reputation of being excellent and as a result ranks highly in a major publication, then its reputation will be enhanced for the next round of reputation surveys. This results in a self-reinforcing process. If the ranking were designed to show the qualities that justify a good reputation, we would not include the actual reputation as a component of the ranking itself.

Additionally, the validity of reputation surveys is highly questionable. The methodology presumes that the academics queried about reputation know something about the many colleges and universities that form part of the survey. In general, it is unlikely that even the best-informed academics have detailed knowledge of the internal operations of even fifty colleges, let alone the thousand involved in these surveys. Even someone who knows ten colleges in detail is not likely to know about changes that take place from year to year, as is implied in the annual questionnaires.

As a result, the reputation results are simply a word-of-mouth notion related to historical prestige. As these rankings have value to alumni and politicians, colleges and universities work hard to show up well in them. They find ways to manipulate the data, and they spend heavily to advertise their colleges in periodicals read by the academic administrators who assign the reputation scores. The goal is to publicize the virtues and significance of relatively lesser-known institutions to improve name recognition and, presumably, reputation.

*Mr. President,* the institutional PR officer says, *we need an advertising blitz in* The Chronicle of Higher Education *and* Inside Higher Ed *to promote our school's innovative programs. What for?* says the president. The PR guy responds, *the* U.S. News *survey will go out to your colleagues soon, and if we want to rank higher we have to get our name out there so others will remember it when filling out the survey. Yes,* the president says, still innocent of the game, *but what have we done that's different from last year that would make our ranking better? Our budget was cut by the state, our student numbers declined, and our football team finished in the middle of the conference.* The PR officer sighs, knowing that there's nothing worse than an honest, straightforward president, and explains, *The issue is not what we've done but what we can tell people we've done. Most people have no idea what we've done, so if we take something good we did, elevate it, present it correctly, and discuss it as a national leadership activity in support of student achievement, we'll get buzz. That buzz will translate into a better* U.S. News *reputation ranking. Oh,* she says, *is that what everyone does? Yes,* he says. *You've seen the ads.* She thinks a moment and then says, *I thought they were real, but if that's the game, I guess we have to play. If you don't,* he says, *your alumni and board will be very unhappy with a reduced ranking.* She asks, *Even if the ranking is worthless?* He patiently explains, *All surveys that rank us high have good methods; those that rank us low are methodologically unsound.*

Nonetheless, in America, ranking is a favorite game, and almost all universities publish good rankings results on their websites even when they know the methodology to be fatally flawed. It is better to be seen as prestigious, they reason, whatever the source of the reputation.

In the special case of the research university, the process is somewhat more complex in one sense and somewhat less arbitrary in another. Academic research is a nationally competitive business where most of the process of awarding grants, securing scholarly publications, and selecting research-related awards of one kind or another is visible to all. Identifying the research institutions is less difficult than finding the top undergraduate colleges. The complexity of research universities, however, makes comprehensive ranking of these institutions difficult.

The most reliable identifier of research preeminence in America is the amount of federally awarded research expenditures of each university each year. As federal agencies award these funds based primarily on peer review, this indicator has validity as representing the research prowess of each institution's faculty and staff.

The *Top American Research Universities* annual reports provide an example of how to develop this form of evaluation. However, as the ranking business spreads overseas, the ranking issues become more complex.

## International Ranking

Universities and nations believe that one of the key elements in the dynamism of American business and industry has been the achievements of its university-based research establishment.

Other countries with research universities work to improve the ones they have, and those without research universities rush to build them.

To mark the success of a national effort to improve research university performance within a global context, a number of international university-ranking projects have emerged. Most of these have a national origin and are designed to match the performance of national universities against the world market for research preeminence.

Absent the unifying structure of the United States federal research funding competition, the international projects look at a number of other variables but usually focus on publications. The notion here is that research requires publication and therefore the number of publications, primarily in scientific journals, can serve as a good comparative indicator of research productivity on an international scale.

However, the academic community does not regard all publications as being equal. Some are more important or significant than others. Not all articles in a journal publication are of equal value: some change the way we think about the world, and others fade into obscurity.

To address this problem, ranking schemes use citation counts that measure the number of times scholars cite a given article. This is seen as a refinement in the methodology, but it also introduces a number of data challenges. Some are ordinary, such as the difficulty of knowing exactly who is who when authors have the same last names and first initials. Some are more complex, such as the difficulty of dealing with disciplines that have papers with many authors and those with just a few. Also, disciplines differ in how they acknowledge authorship. Some will list authors in alphabetical order while others put the primary author first or last. In some fields, the authorship will include all the participants on a project, not just the authors of the paper. These different customs for acknowledging authorship complicate the process of evaluating citations and publication productivity.

Sometimes the issue of where the citation is made becomes significant. If an article is cited many times but by authors who publish in second-tier publications, should it count as much as an article cited fewer times but by authors who publish in premier publications? Moreover, how do we determine the premier and the secondary publications?

Some international ranking schemes use reputation surveys to enhance their publications, but here too the problem of circularity appears. If we all know that Oxford is a great university, but we do not know much about the University of Queensland in Australia, how valid can our impressions of reputation be?

The recent appearance of the Global Research Benchmarking System (GRBS) has addressed these issues in an effective and creative way and raised the quality and significance of international ranking based on publications and citations. The considerable literature on ranking issues and validity is well worth reading, but whatever the system, the enormous pressure to produce and show well on these rankings indicates the great importance the world places on the performance of research universities.

*Chapter 5*

# Teaching

-------------------------------------------------------------------

Almost all American universities begin with teaching. Research universities have a major commitment to the exploration and development of new knowledge, but most organize their work from a base in teaching. The scale of the teaching mission can range from the undergraduate enrollment of a private research university such as Cal Tech, with about 950 students, to the student population of a large public research university such as the Ohio State University, with about 41,000 undergraduate students.

The ratio between graduate students and undergraduates and the balance of instructional programs between the liberal arts and sciences versus applied disciplines and the professions also differ significantly from campus to campus and from private to public institution. These characteristics of the teaching environment help establish differences in campus culture and style. In almost all cases, however, teaching matters in American research universities, as it does in all of postsecondary education.

Teaching is a subject near and dear to everyone's heart. All observers of colleges believe they understand teaching because most of them have experienced teaching as students, teachers, or both. Although they may not agree with each other, academics and everyone else believe they know the essential elements of good teaching, and most have firm opinions about the proper outcome of instruction.

Teaching is an accessible art and practice. People can see what teachers do, observe the process, and experience its impact. This leads to a wide range of opinions on the benefits, content, characteristics, and outcomes of teaching. If these opinions coincided, the work of the university would be much easier, but they do not.

Every educational learning fad finds its passionate adherents within and without the university, advocates who believe that some particular technique, approach, incentive, or behavior on the part of teachers or students will bring about greatly enhanced learning. This enthusiasm reflects the popular belief that university teaching delivers great value and deserves careful attention. Several themes recur in the endless conversation about teaching. Some of these are part of the discussion about the productivity and quality of teaching. Here we think a bit about the content of teaching.

## Content of Teaching

As we would expect from the pragmatic history of American colleges and universities, instruction has an academic perspective and a practical delivery mechanism. Universities mostly adhere to a general, if not too precise, standard notion of what constitutes a "liberal" or arts-and-sciences education, and they express this standard through the structure of the undergraduate curriculum. This core content, though the subject of sometimes intense intellectual and cultural debate, is actually quite stable and relatively uniform throughout American higher education.

Some will protest that the curriculum ignores the classics (however defined); misses new authors and overemphasizes or underemphasizes some cultural, international, or political perspective; does not do enough for foreign languages or for math and the sciences; or neglects other critical topics. Yet, in truth, the differences among universities reflect mostly style and labeling rather than substance, as a sampling from websites of the curricula of quite different types of colleges and universities will show.

The similarity of college curricula comes from the twin power of competition and regulation. Competition ensures that each college and university offers much the same curriculum to a common marketplace of students and parents seeking equivalent products. In competing for students, most institutions focus on minor forms of product differentiation, image, and presentation.

Regulation reinforces this standardization of content through accreditation, a process that encourages or coerces colleges and universities to deliver remarkably similar undergraduate programs. This regulation is even more significant for applied and professional programs, whose accreditation groups often enforce detailed content and delivery specifications.

Teaching, the individual practice of instruction, receives much attention and study. Not all of this helps. Academics know that teaching is a handicraft activity in which an instructor engages students so the students will learn what the instructor knows they need to learn.

Good teaching delivers both informational content (names, dates, facts, formulas) and methodological process (critical thinking, analytical techniques, and information evaluation, validation, and verification). Good teaching gives the student methodological and analytical skills that extend beyond the current validity of the informational content.

Since teaching is a joint handicraft process between an individual student and a teacher, the instruction that works for one teacher-student combination and subject matter may not work equally well for another combination. Successful teaching in large groups uses different styles and techniques than teaching in small groups. Online, interactive, large lectures, small seminars: no single, uniform methodology for teaching works for all subjects, students, teachers, or classes. This provides a basis for a significant literature and controversy on the styles, techniques, and results of teaching.

Because academics know much about teaching, they often find the public conversation about teaching and learning frustrating. Some observers of the undergraduate experience, unhappy with the results of college instruction, seek to shift the conversation to something they call "learning" and place this notion outside the process of teaching. Teaching, in this view, is simply a mechanical process; learning, however, is the real thing, the product of teaching.

Many faculty believe that the two are the same thing: if we succeed in teaching, the results of the course, as reflected in the grades, indicate individual students' learning. Reformers, seeking to weaken the authority of the teacher, create external measures of teaching effectiveness and call that "learning." Unfortunately, learning is no less an individualized product and no less dependent on the perspective of the student than is the teaching that produces the learning.

The American enthusiasm for self-realization and the individual's sense of well-being leads many to focus on students' beliefs about what they may have learned. We can ask a student, "Do you feel that you learned? How did your experiences outside the classroom or in service projects help you learn?"

Because the actual learning that takes place is individualized, students learn for themselves and not for others. Nonetheless, much evaluation emphasizes the process of teaching, as if by knowing the process we could certify the learning. In the quantitative fields of the sciences, math, and technology, learning is more easily tested, and specialized learning systems and self-paced, technology-mediated instruction often prove effective. In the cognitive fields of the social sciences and humanities or the performance instruction of the fine arts, learning is more individualized and less effectively measured with standardized testing.

Most universities manage undergraduate teaching through the specification of a structured academic content that includes some standard patterns. Almost all colleges and universities identify two dimensions in the undergraduate academic content: core requirements and a major.

The *core requirements* speak to the virtually universal commitment of American higher education to providing students with a general understanding of the content and analytical process of disciplines in the sciences, the humanities, and the social sciences. Often these requirements go under the name "General Education," or, in student parlance, "GenEd."

The *major* recognizes the requirement to know what it means to be an expert, to understand the dimensions of a particular field of study, and to recognize how experts in this field acquire and master knowledge. While few expect the information acquired in the major to remain current and useful for a lifetime, everyone expects the skills learned in acquiring that major to remain useful indefinitely and to serve as a student's permanent, core tools for learning.

A major is the defining purpose of the college degree, and the question put to most students by their friends and relatives is "What's your major?" This focus on the major reflects recognition that while general knowledge is valuable, and while knowing how the world works is an asset, success in today's world is driven by expertise. The major introduces students to the criteria and process for achieving expertise even if the major is usually not sufficient to create a true expert.

## Organization of Teaching

If we find consistent structures for the curricula maintained by most colleges and universities, the actual organization and management of the delivery of instruction varies greatly by size of institution. In small, elite liberal arts colleges, the resident faculty deliver the curriculum in classes that may vary from five to twenty students up to as many as eighty to a hundred for survey courses. The students and faculty often know each other well by the end of the four-year experience. The curriculum is standardized for all students, with relatively few alternative paths to a degree, but nonetheless offers multiple opportunities for tailoring academic programs to individual student interests.

The value provided in this structure is the personal and direct interaction of students and faculty over time. This mode of instruction tends to be labor intensive and thus expensive. If the college has national-quality faculty and state-of-the-art facilities, students and their parents will see high tuition and other costs, and even then the college will need to subsidize this teaching style from endowment earnings.

Most institutions delivering instruction in this format exist in the private sector, and many have a historical or current sectarian character. Colleges with this style have enrollments from one thousand (the bare minimum for institutional survival in most cases) to perhaps five thousand (the transition point beyond which colleges may become too large to sustain the intimate style).

In larger institutions, now almost always called universities whatever their academic character, the faculty teach undergraduates in large and small classes, but additional part-time, adjunct, or graduate student teachers, some with subprofessorial credentials, take over parts of the instructional and academic support functions. In large institutions, these non–tenure track faculty (often called contingent faculty to recognize that their employment is contingent on the institution's immediate needs) may teach survey courses and beginning language or math courses and manage science laboratories.

Some universities have had significant success implementing computer-driven teaching systems for lower-level courses in math and English that adapt to widely different student preparation and learning progress. They may also deploy distance-education platforms to enhance the flexibility and extend the reach of their instructional programs.

Class sizes in big institutions range from 15-20 to 500 (or more for some general lecture survey courses). In these larger institutions, students can lose the opportunity for intimate and continuous academic interaction with a small group of faculty, but they gain access to a large pool of expert faculty in an extensive array of specialties. Students have many alternative paths to different degree specializations, and they can make many choices to enhance or customize their course of study.

The management of enrollment and instruction at large universities, particularly as the scale rises from the 5,000-10,000 undergraduate students to the 30,000-50,000 category, requires significant managerial and technical skill to put students in the right classes at the right time with the right instructor. Managing the teaching process of a large institution takes time, attention, and expertise.

In all institutions, large or small, technology serves to enhance and modify traditional forms of instruction. Video and other electronic media provide alternative content for some courses, substituting for books and lectures. Computer-mediated instruction and various forms of distance and continuing education modify and enhance instructional patterns in most universities, and institutions will surely increase the deployment of these technologies over the next decades.

Technology will indeed be a significant driver of higher education forms and function, but the balance between cost and effectiveness is still unclear. Under some circumstances, distance education functions effectively, but not under all. Computerized instructional support systems have great promise but require careful planning, design, and implementation for effective results. As the technology becomes more stable and standardized, adoption across the industry will likely increase.

Textbooks also appear to be in transition, as the high cost of many print books creates an opportunity for an alternative market for Internet-delivered media, extensive used-book secondary markets, development and distribution of e-books, and other commercial readjustments to the book business. Students, of course, adopt new technology faster than their faculty, and the use of Facebook, Twitter, text messaging, and Internet-based research creates a host of challenges and opportunities for new instructional approaches.

However, as all seasoned administrators know, new technology always has great promise but also high transition costs. The best advice is usually to let rich institutions or those with special expertise or circumstances experiment and identify the most effective new modes of instruction. Enthusiasm for riding the wild waves of technological innovation is contagious, but it is often resisted by wise university leaders, who wait until the experience of others in the marketplace permits a realistic cost-benefit analysis.

*I read about a terrific Internet program for teaching students online in* USA Today *this morning,* says the enthusiastic trustee. *Why aren't we doing this? All the important universities are doing it. We should get going. Yes,* says the wise president, *those are very interesting programs, and we are constantly evaluating them to see when it will be best to engage. The sooner the better,* says the trustee. *We don't want to be left behind.* The president wants to say, *Give me a break!* USA Today *looks for hot topics, not good programs. Yes, fancy Internet options are everywhere, but we can't do them all, we shouldn't do them all, and we should always see what they cost. This one in the newspaper costs too much, has no proven track record of success, and has no business model for recovering the cost in any reasonable amount of time.* Since trustees are often uninterested in hearing views other than their own, the president proceeds with caution, knowing that another trendy innovation may well appear next month, promoted by a different trustee.

*Graduate instruction,* an especially important function in large research universities, has its own characteristics. Graduate classroom instruction mirrors undergraduate teaching, although at a higher level of intensity and a higher expectation of performance. The size of graduate classroom instruction scales from ten to eighty students per class, with most classes near the lower end. The permanent faculty deliver large parts of the MA/MS and professional graduate curricula in this mode.

*Seminars, colloquia, laboratory-based projects, and thesis/dissertation activity* focus on research. They are critical components of some master's-level and professional curricula and are essential parts of PhD programs. Instruction in this mode involves the faculty and students in groups ranging from one to twenty members.

Regardless of institutional size, most advanced graduate education falls to the regular faculty or to distinguished, fully qualified visiting or part-time faculty. Often, external observers greatly underestimate the time and attention required to produce a PhD graduate in many fields. In the sciences, the attention devoted to PhD instruction is individualized and intense over a long period. Students require equipment and laboratories; they need the support and funding that an established faculty member's laboratory and projects can provide.

Humanities and social sciences faculty pay close attention to their PhD students to ensure that their projects are well designed, that the materials required are accessible, and that the final product will be publishable. All of this is handicraft labor, and so far, there are no technological or other mechanisms to create economies of scale.

Clearly, then, scale of operation has the most impact on undergraduate teaching and the least on graduate instruction. Graduate teaching gains least from economies of scale, either through reduced labor costs or through the efficient use of facilities or technology. Undergraduate instruction gains the most from economies of scale in all areas, from labor through facilities and technology.

The fixed cost of graduate education, especially above the master's-degree level and for many professional degrees, responds hardly at all to issues of scale. Indeed, the principal costs of advanced graduate education come from the support and maintenance of the research enterprise within which graduate education takes place. This issue of scale helps explain why both public and private research universities appear most similar in their graduate and PhD education and least similar in their undergraduate programs.

Special circumstances apply to graduate professional education in the health sciences and other fields with specific regulatory requirements. External accreditation agencies for these programs often specify the resources required for each student so rigidly that few economies of scale are possible. Indeed, institutions must have the money to purchase the minimum requirements to sustain these degree programs. Absent the funds to buy equipment, hire the required number of faculty and professional staff, and provide the space and other resources required by the accreditation agency, the university cannot offer the program.

Universities manage their teaching responsibilities by attempting to meet the academic standards demanded by the faculty; the learning expectations of students, parents, and employers; and the cultural expectations of the supporting public. Managing instruction is one of the university's principal challenges.

## Chapter 6

# Research

--------------------------------------------------------------------

Research defines the character and the quality of research universities. Even when research institutions teach thousands of undergraduate students, the quality of their faculty and the breadth and depth of their programs—graduate or undergraduate—depend on the research enterprise. This does not mean that the undergraduate program exists subordinate to research activities, only that the quality of university research drives the quality, breadth, and depth of the undergraduate curriculum.

The common mantra of almost all major universities speaks to teaching and research in the same breath, as if they were similar things, but they are not. Teaching and research use related but different talents, address different audiences, and focus on the academic enterprise in different ways.

Research seeks the unknown and pursues knowledge at the boundaries of our current understanding. Teaching delivers the state of current knowledge. Research, by virtue of the expertise required for reaching beyond what we know, tends to focus narrowly and deeply. Teaching, by virtue of its mission to deliver what we already know, focuses more broadly and generally.

More important for understanding the university, teaching talent is more common than research talent. This realization engenders tremendous unhappiness on the part of all of us who teach. We teachers want to believe that what we do requires the rarest of talents. Teaching, a difficult and demanding activity requiring intelligence and understanding, rests on talents found widely among academics.

Talent capable of sustaining quality research productivity for many years occurs much less frequently, is much more fragile, and demands a much higher level of institutional management and support. Research is both labor- and materials-intensive, requiring not only the best talent available in the world but also libraries, laboratories, equipment, computers, assistants, and other elements that support the creativity of the faculty researcher (or creative artist, in the case of the fine and performing arts and some humanities).

Because research talent is scarce, it is expensive. Because it is fragile, it may not last for an academic lifetime. Research careers of talented faculty may continue for as many as forty years or for as few as five or ten. The longevity of a highly productive faculty research career depends on many things: intelligence, inspiration, determination, opportunity, funding, creativity, and luck. Hard work helps, but alone it does not guarantee that a research program will produce good results. If creativity and inspiration misfire, not all the hard work in the world will produce a significant research result.

## Research Competition

Research is also among the most highly competitive enterprises in America. Research scholars, whatever their field, compete for the money that supports their work and for recognition of the quality and significance of their discoveries.

Even poets, whose work requires little money and no elaborate infrastructure, nonetheless must compete with all the other poets for recognition of the quality of their poetry through publication in significant places. If a poet fails to win that recognition and peers and critics find the poems lacking in originality, insight, or distinction, then the poet's creative work fails.

This is the peer review to which all researchers must submit, either for the support of grant agencies whose funds make the research possible or for the publication opportunity that permits colleagues in the field worldwide to review the research or creative results. Every element of a research project's or creative activity's design and product receives critical review, and critics quickly find any defects in design or results.

Quality researchers who have substantial achievements over time command high salaries and significant funding from their universities. They exist in a competitive marketplace where institutions will bid for their services and drive up their price.

Research, being the leading product of the university and the source of all that we eventually teach, enjoys first rank in American research universities. Even the high-quality liberal arts college, dedicated to a teaching mission, will encourage, support, and highlight the research accomplishments of its faculty.

Managing research enterprises within a large university takes careful attention. These enterprises require funding, space, equipment, libraries, and technical support. They generate special legal and management issues. Research, because of its high value to the university and to society, attracts public attention. Universities compete on the amount of research they do, for the funds required to support this research, and for the opportunity to commercialize its results.

Research is a national and international concern, drawing the attention and interest of experts and the public around the world. Teaching is of local importance to an institution because it affects only one institution's students. Teaching, if it is spectacularly good, will be good only for those students taught locally. Research, if it is good, will change the way the world works, affect the teaching and research of faculty and students everywhere, attract the attention of governments and industries, and bring great opportunities and risks to the institution.

## Managing Research

Given this importance, universities create dedicated offices to promote, regulate, monitor, and manage the research activity of their faculty. They identify and attract funding and manage the space, equipment, and operational needs of researchers. They protect the faculty and guide them in meeting extensive and complex regulatory requirements. They ensure that the value of the intellectual property created by research is commercialized properly for the benefit of the university, the nation, the state, public institutions, and the faculty member.

Issues of science, humanities, social sciences, and the arts involve state and national, and sometimes international, policy and practice. Research universities maintain alliances and engagements with political and policy actors to ensure that the interests of university research receive appropriate attention and proper government support. As the previous discussion on ranking research universities makes clear, nations see the research university as a powerful base for achieving their national aspirations.

Research is a resource-intensive enterprise that derives its funding from many sources. Most universities spend the majority of their institutional resources on teaching and expect the faculty to generate much of the revenue needed to underwrite research from grants and contracts. At the same time, universities know that grants and contracts will not pay the full cost of research.

For example, a midlevel public research university might spend about $160 million on research. Of that amount, some $95 million comes from grants and contracts awarded by state, federal, and private agencies. The remaining $65 million comes from state general appropriations, student fees, endowment earnings, gifts from individuals, and other income.

While teaching dollars come in regularly and predictably based on relatively stable enrollments with their attendant state support and tuition dollars, research funding requires constant and successful competition in the marketplace to earn the revenue from contracts and grants necessary for the survival of the research enterprise. In the contest for external research support, universities must invest more of the funds generated from other sources to support successful programs that produce higher amounts of external funding. As mentioned earlier, research income from grants and contracts never covers the full cost of performing the research. While universities receive funds that should cover the indirect overhead costs of heat, light, library, computing, and other infrastructure, most universities are fortunate if they recover half of the audited indirect costs of research allowed by government regulations.

The additional necessary support comes from the investment of the university's internal funds (whether acquired from state appropriations, tuition and fees, sales and services, or endowment income and gifts) and allows the institution to increase the scale of its research activity. Scale is important, because the more research accomplished the greater success the institution will have in acquiring the highest-quality faculty and the largest share of research grants. But even at the highest-performing research universities, external funding does not pay the full cost of research.

For the major private and public research universities, nothing matters more than the successful management of this difficult but critical element of their enterprises. Research is hard to do, difficult to sustain, and essential to the institution's identity and success, although sometimes our constituency finds the research enterprise a bit difficult to understand.

*You know,* my favorite sports booster says, *this research stuff your faculty do is really a boondoggle. Why is that?* I ask. *Well,* he says, *let's look at football. We play the game and maybe a hundred thousand people come, either inside or outside tailgating, millions watch on television, and at the end of the day we know whether we won or lost. At the end of the year, either we're champions or not. Now,* he continues, *you research people, you spend a fortune on fancy equipment and laboratories. The faculty work on their little projects, and many don't even teach. At the end of the year, if they're good, they write up an article that only ten people in the world understand, and when their project finishes, there's usually nothing to show: no product, no machine, nothing but expense and obsolete equipment. Then you guys subsidize this research person to do it all over again. Makes no sense.* Giving nothing to my sports-crazed alum, I say, *If it weren't for research, old people like you and me wouldn't still be alive, our iPhones wouldn't exist, and our CD players wouldn't work. Those are all practical consequences of research. Oh sure,* he answers, *you get a few good things, but you waste tons of time and money on dumb, bizarre ideas that never produce anything. Perhaps,* I say, *but the thing is, research is about what we don't know, so often we're wrong. But when we're right, which we don't know ahead of time, we change the world. Maybe,* he says, *but the kickoff is soon. I need to get to my skybox, because football is an investment I understand and can enjoy now.*

## Chapter 7

# Faculty

-------------------------------------------------------

Faculty represent a capital asset of the university. Following a business model, we might imagine that the buildings, equipment, books, and other tangible goods represent the university's capital assets, and they do, of course. However, the university understands these traditional capital assets better if it sees them as essential elements supporting the faculty.

Students like to believe that they are the reason for the university, but this is not so. Students come to the university because of the faculty, and without the faculty, no university would exist. Moreover, faculty drive the largest part of the cost of any institution of higher education. Some costs appear directly through salaries and fringe benefits, but many more come indirectly through libraries, laboratories, classrooms, offices, staff support, and other goods and services required for faculty productivity.

The industrial model that sees faculty primarily as labor does not accurately capture the importance of faculty within the university's activity. Faculty, in this business view, simply represent some form of knowledge worker, and in response to economic difficulties many faculty take advantage of this misconception to construct labor unions that reinforce the mistaken notion. Faculty may require a union under some circumstances to protect themselves against an institution's corporate-style labor and wage policies, but the existence of the union simply overlays the cost of its bureaucracy on top of the institutional cost of managing faculty capital assets.

Capital is the best way to characterize faculty because tenured faculty represent a long-term investment not easily transferred, repurposed, sold, or otherwise liquidated. Faculty, hired to teach and do research, achieve tenure after their sixth year at most institutions, and they then become as permanent an institutional investment as most buildings. Faculty careers may run for thirty or forty years, and the university carries an obligation to pay for this asset and its attendant costs at some reasonable level regardless of its productivity or its contribution to the institutional mission.

As is the case with many physical assets, management cannot easily transfer faculty functions from an original purpose to a new purpose. If the original purpose becomes uneconomic, obsolete, or otherwise unneeded by the institution, the faculty assets associated with that purpose do not simply flow into another more productive use. As might happen for factory production lines constructed for a now-obsolete purpose, a change in function for a faculty member implies significant new costs, if the retooling is even possible.

Like many buildings on the historic register, faculty who no longer serve an economic purpose can only be reconstructed at such a high cost that it is often more efficient to buy a new faculty member than to reconstruct an old one. In this circumstance, the institution pays the extra cost of maintaining obsolete professors rather than incur the political and social costs of removing them from the payroll.

This characteristic of the faculty comes from the specialized nature of their expertise. Historians do not teach chemistry, Elizabethan scholars do not teach Spanish, and engineers do not teach sculpture. Each faculty guild, especially in research institutions, has strict requirements for entry and permanent status, and generalists tend to disappear from the employment stream before receiving tenure, if they were ever allowed to enter.

In most cases, the investment in the capital asset of faculty proves wise, and the faculty continue to deliver good returns on any investment made in their careers throughout their useful professional lifetimes. Nonetheless, no one engaged in the management of universities should ever think of faculty as a work force; they are the university's most important capital asset.

Faculty also represent institutional capital because a university's mission, purpose, and goals succeed or fail on the basis of its investment in them. The administrators, staff, buildings, students, and alumni do not create the value of the university. They contribute to it and support it, but the astute investment in the capital asset of faculty produces the institution's value to its constituencies and owners.

Being highly individualistic in temperament and each possessing a specific and virtually unique set of skills, individual faculty may not welcome the perspective that sees them as part of an aggregate capital asset. They are right in this attitude, for the management of faculty is an individualized art, as any department chair will only too eagerly explain.

Our interest here is to identify the structure of faculty life and careers. Only by understanding the way faculty interact with their institutions and their guilds can universities improve their operations.

## Promotion and Tenure

Faculty, along with their supporters and critics, spend time and energy on the analysis of promotion and tenure. These topics elicit much controversy but often for the wrong reasons.

*Promotion* recognizes cumulative accomplishment at various levels of guild-established productivity and quality.

*Tenure* represents the institution's permanent investment in and the guild's judgment of the future productivity and accomplishments of a faculty candidate.

While many critics worry that tenure protects the incompetent and subversive, this is not the major issue for the university and its guilds. Very few tenured faculty prove to be incompetent. Instead, the issue is more subtle and complex.

Universities have only a fixed amount of faculty capital investment to spend on the production of quality. A professor whose productivity and quality decline represents a less-than-optimal use of the institution's resources. The test of optimal use is whether the university could get a better faculty member in the market using the same amount of money invested in a current faculty member.

Positive tenure decisions represent a bet by the guild and the institution that the long-term investment in faculty members will deliver a high value over their professional lifetimes, a value that is as good as or better than any other investment in faculty members that the institution could make. The decision about tenure is much more important than the decision about promotion. Promotion sets standards of achievement at several points in a career for all members of a guild, but by awarding tenure, the university makes a one-time decision about a long-term investment of scarce capital in an asset that the institution expects will produce nationally competitive quality over a lifetime of service.

These decisions (which set the standards of cumulative performance through promotion and make the institution's capital investment in future performance through tenure) are of such importance that faculty and administrators create elaborate validating procedures. The process of promotion and tenure represents a form of academic due diligence similar to what a business employs when deciding whether to acquire another company, a new plant, or new equipment. In the academic world, the process is no less formalized, no less rigorous, and overall, no less effective in making good decisions than in the business world. The added complication in the academic world is that these decisions directly involve specific individuals, not inanimate physical or financial objects.

Tenure evaluation in particular represents a life-challenging experience for the candidate. For this reason, faculty advocates tend to develop complex bureaucratic measures to protect candidates against negative decisions in these processes. Only the most rigorous research universities use a decision process that measures a tenure candidate directly against comparable quality available in the external marketplace.

In most universities, the process is biased in favor of the candidate. This bias works through a definition of satisfactory continuous work. If a faculty member does a good job, a job that meets the minimum or at best the average standards of the local guild, then the presumption is that the institution will make the permanent investment and grant tenure.

In the most rigorous research universities, which are mostly private, the standard measures the candidate against the market. These institutions ask this question: "Is a lifetime investment in tenure for this candidate the highest and best use of the institution's funds?" Or, more specifically, "Can the university find a better person in the marketplace for this position than the candidate before us, regardless of whether the current faculty member has performed up to the generally accepted standard for the profession?"

*How do I get tenure?* my new colleague, fresh out of a good graduate school with a recently completed PhD, asks. *Well,* I respond, *our rules say you have to be excellent in two and at least good in one of the three categories of faculty work: teaching, research, and service. What do I concentrate on?* he asks. *That's easy,* I say. *You do all of them, but you recognize the differences.*

*You can be a good teacher tomorrow by preparing well today. You can provide good service by participating today. But you can't have good research results by the fifth year unless you are working today to have your work published and recognized by year five. Time is the enemy of research productivity. Wow, that's tough,* he says. *Yes,* I say, *that's because the reward for research is delayed until long after the work is done while the feedback for teaching and service is now. Resist the reinforcement of super teaching and the siren song of community service; instead, do the research. No one believes in a promise of research, only in the demonstration of published results.* My colleague thinks I'm a cynical old fogey, but the other faculty in the department say, *Yes he is, but he's also right.*

A reading of the formal documents that support and define faculty personnel policies and practices provides a useful perspective on the complexity and formality of the promotion and tenure practices of American universities, both public and private. Additionally, the commentary available from the website of the principal organization that defends the tenure rights and responsibilities of faculty (the American Association of University Professors) and one of the more aggressive trade union representatives of faculty employees gives a sense of the profession's focus on sustaining the tenure rights established in current practice.

Universities often address the concern about sustained faculty performance after tenure and promotion to full professor status by instituting a post-tenure review process. Occurring perhaps every fourth to sixth year, the process reviews accomplishments in teaching and research since the previous review measured against guild standards. If the faculty member's performance is subpar, a plan for improvement can be established. Theoretically, sequential poor reviews could lead to dismissal, although that is a rare occurrence.

For very senior faculty, the prospect of a negative post-tenure review can, however, encourage a discussion about retirement. Post-tenure review has been most commonly implemented as a formal activity by public universities, although some private institutions also participate. Primarily a defense against attacks on tenure, these post-tenure review processes can, if done systematically, become expensive and time consuming. The actual real value of these reviews beyond public relations is unclear.

## Contingent and Contract Faculty

The significance of the tenure investment and the risks it entails often encourage universities to rent faculty rather than incur the risk and future costs of permanently hiring tenured faculty. While few universities support a continuing large group of nontenured full-time faculty, most rent part-time faculty in ever-increasing numbers, creating a category of what we now call contingent faculty.

The inflexibility of a full-time tenure-track faculty investment has led many institutions to use industrial labor models when employing teaching and even research personnel. These contingent faculty, part-time or full-time non–tenure-track employees, are often fully qualified with PhD training, publications, and teaching experience, but the university or college chooses to hire them on temporary contracts for specific purposes rather than making a long-term commitment to them.

This technique gives the institution the ability to immediately adjust the financial commitment to faculty personnel in response to budget changes or variations in student interest or demand. Contingent contracts allow the institution to manage faculty in accord with short-term faculty productivity. If a contingent faculty member is not teaching at a high enough level of quality and quantity, the institution can hire someone else.

Similarly, some parts of the academic research enterprise employ significant numbers of contract research faculty whose job is to do research, get grants, and otherwise be productive. If they fail to perform or their specialty becomes obsolete, they can be replaced with more suitable research personnel.

The tenure-track faculty have considerable difficulty deciding how to deal with contingent faculty, and the contingent faculty themselves have their own issues with this system. Tenure-track faculty understand that the increasing use of non–tenure-track faculty means a reduction in the importance of tenure to the university. They also know that the use of contingent faculty may mean that in a financially constrained environment, the contingent faculty will be the first to go, preserving the continuity of the tenured staff. Most faculty argue for making all positions tenure-track to ensure strong defense of their own property rights in tenure.

Contingent faculty have differing perspectives on this issue. For some, the freedom from having to meet tenure requirements in the up-or-out atmosphere of most university tenure processes, especially at research-intensive institutions, is an advantage. They see themselves as good at what they do (teaching, for example) and do not want to have to engage in research or service.

Others, of course, worry about the job insecurity of contingent status. In many instances, especially for part-time faculty, the benefits are poor. Collegial life for contingent or contract faculty can be disappointing, and the actual responsibilities of full-time contingent faculty remain somewhat variable (Do they perform service? Do they vote on instructional issues? Can they serve on research committees?).

As the number of contingent faculty rises to over half the total number of faculty employed in all types of United States colleges and universities, institutions are likely to pay closer attention to standardizing the context for these instructional and research faculty.

## Chapter 8

# Finance

-----------------------------------------------------------

While most university conversations focus on issues of academic substance—program content, research results, and curriculum issues, for example—almost every conversation carries a subtext about money. Universities use special words to describe money questions. They talk about "resources" or "program support" when what they actually mean is "money." Part of this reluctance to talk directly and clearly about money comes from the organizational model of the undergraduate college.

In an undergraduate college, students take courses in the humanities, social sciences, and sciences. Their majors differ from physics to fine arts, from American literature to political science. The college usually charges all students the same tuition regardless of the cost of the programs or courses they take.

In this model, the college distributes its money not in relation to what individual departments earn but primarily in relation to the cost of the academic design of the curriculum. As a result, the key issue about money is indirect. If a guild's academic specialties are central to the college's academic design, the college will pay for them. The guilds, recognizing this, spend their time arguing about academic design. This makes the conversation sound philosophical and academic, but it is actually also a surrogate conversation about the distribution of money.

Faculty, too, prefer to think of their work as mostly unconnected to money, although they have strong opinions about the importance of a living wage. Many academic people express their disdain toward the issue of money rather inconsistently. Most faculty do not think that the university should be driven by financial issues and dislike the notion of the university as "business," but most faculty also think that the university's money should be spent on their priorities for "support."

Indeed, the faculty expect the institution (through its administrative shell) to find the necessary resources (money). The faculty also assume it is their obligation to criticize the internal distribution of those resources without necessarily assuming an obligation to increase the university's ability to earn money or to fully understand the financial structure of the institution. These attitudes operate in the abstract, for in real time and with real people, faculty are as carefully clear about money as anyone else. Faculty know what things cost, they know what the university pays other professors like themselves, they know what it costs to attract a graduate student, and they know how much it will take to set up a research laboratory. What they often do not know and frequently choose to ignore is the structure of the university's finances.

This ignorance is variable and often encouraged by administrators. If the faculty do not understand the financial structure of the university, they will surely criticize everything the administration does, but administrators will find it relatively easy to deflect this poorly informed criticism.

## Financial Reporting

University financial reporting contributes to this state of useful confusion by focusing on the management of individual funds, or pots of money, and not directly on the income and expenses of the institution. This fund accounting can complicate university understanding because it obscures the key relationships among the income sources and expenses associated with university work. It makes the underlying financial structure of the institution and its programs less obvious than would other forms of financial accounting prevalent in commercial business enterprises.

Universities, as not-for-profit organizations, do not focus on reporting how much profit they make during the year. Instead, universities must tell various organizations and individuals how the institution used the money that came from each identifiable source. Universities provide an accounting of their overall financial health and generate Statements of Net Assets similar to traditional balance sheets and other financial documents, but they organize their account books primarily around specific funds designated for particular purposes.

For example, if a donor gives money to support student scholarships, the university must put that money in an identifiable fund. Then, each year, the university makes an accounting of that specific fund to determine whether the university spent the donor's money on student scholarships. If the university spent the money on scholarships, it satisfies the fund accounting requirements. If the university has a fund for salaries, it must spend the dollars in that fund on salaries; if it has a fund for purchasing equipment, it must spend the money on equipment. At the end of the day, the university accountants can demonstrate that the institution followed the rules that define all its funds and that it spent the money available in each fund on things for which the fund exists. This is all good.

Unfortunately, this approach lacks a straightforward system for understanding the relationship between spending money and achieving the university's goals. Did the scholarships bring in better students? Did the equipment help faculty get grants or students learn? The university can take a second step to link expenditures to specific results, but it is not required to do so.

Fund accounting can also make it difficult to understand the cost of the various university actions. Often a given activity, say, the history department, will spend money from several funds. A calculation of the true cost of the history department's work becomes a challenge since the accounting is organized by fund, not by activity.

Although fund accounting does not prevent universities from understanding their finances, it does not require them to do so. Furthermore, because universities do not make a profit and do not sell shares in the marketplace, they have less incentive to create standard categories of income and expense related to productivity or quality that could permit comparative analysis.

Take the example of teaching and research. Every major university does both teaching and research (although in varying proportions depending on its mission). It is of considerable interest to know how much of the university's income goes to support teaching and how much goes to support research. Universities often report a number that appears to indicate how much the university spends on instruction. We might believe that this number accurately represents teaching expenses and even do some analysis based on that belief. We would be wrong to do so.

The rules used to allocate an expenditure to teaching or research or advising or some other function are implemented by the university's financial officers accurately, but classification standards for universities may not all match. Some institutions have sophisticated methods for allocating an individual faculty member's time between teaching and research, which may allow for a reasonably accurate accounting of the investment in teaching or research. Others may allocate based on tradition or judgment. The cost of department-funded research, for example, reflects the cost of faculty time not allocated to specific teaching responsibilities, administrative duties, or other defined purposes and not paid by an external grant or contract. It is almost a residual after accounting for explicit assignments. A university may have an accurate understanding of its expenses on teaching and research at the lowest level of detail, but the different methods of reporting these costs at each institution make the comparative analysis of teaching and research expenses among institutions difficult.

In public universities, significant portions of the money spent on university activities may not even appear in the university's books or may appear in separate reports. For example, some university foundations that hold the endowment and annual-giving accounts exist as separate agencies. The substantial sums they spend to support faculty salaries, fellowships, or other university expenses sometimes appear in the university's financial statements as separate items if they are large enough, but they may not all be captured as part of the general accounting of the university. Some costs, such as those related to intercollegiate athletics, may not all be included in the university's reports; other activities, such as legal services, some financial services, and even campus planning services, may not appear as costs to the university because they take place in a state-level office.

Many universities do not have a clear understanding of capital costs. Universities usually finance their facilities through borrowing, and the related debt service is a major financial item. The methods for reporting this university-related debt vary. In some public institutions, capital debt is carried by the state and does not appear on university accounts at all. Some building projects rely on earmarked funds from state or federal agencies. Others combine money from donor gifts, debt financing, and other sources to pay for construction. It is usually better to build with the money in hand rather than through borrowing. In addition, the requirements for operations and maintenance costs for new facilities and the creation of funds to pay for required renovations over the usually long life spans of academic buildings vary. In some places, athletic debt may be carried by an affiliated foundation, whereas other universities report it directly as an institutional obligation.

These variations reflect the different histories and political or financial structures of institutions. While there is nothing improper or incorrect about these differences, they often make comparative analysis of university finance unreliable.

## All-Funds Accounting

The essential starting point for all conversations about university finance is a complete accounting for all funds used for university work, whatever their source. This all-funds accounting, which might appear obvious at first inspection, is sometimes difficult to achieve, especially at public universities. The more complex and sophisticated the university, the more difficult will be the construction of an all-funds budget or financial statement.

The CFO comes in to meet the new chancellor and asks, *What information do you need?* The new chancellor says, *Do we have a good summary of our financial circumstances?* The CFO says, *Sure, here it is.* The chancellor, wise to the ways of university financial thinking, checks the figures and then says, *Is this all the money?* The CFO looks puzzled and says, *Yes, see, we receive $400 million from the state, and this shows how we get it.* She asks, *Where's the tuition and fee money?* Oh, says the CFO, *that's on another sheet with all the fee revenue.* She asks, *And what about the money from endowment earnings and annual giving? Yes,* says the CFO, *we can get that from the foundation.* She then asks, *And where is the grant and contract revenue?* Oh, he says, *that's in the research office under sponsored programs, but we can get it.* Relentlessly moving on, she says, *What about residence halls and parking?* He scrambles for cover. *Sure, but those are auxiliary enterprises.* She follows with, *And do we have any debt service?* He answers, *Of course,* *but that's in the capital accounts. Well, says the chancellor, can you try to get all the money on one sheet so I can see what we have? Then we can look at where it goes. OK, says the CFO, eager to get out of range, but it may take some time since no one has ever asked for that before.*

In public universities, the regulatory and political structures that surround institutions force the invention of many creative and complicated mechanisms to hold dollars that do not come from state treasuries or from tax-based sources. To evade regulatory controls, public universities can construct foundations separate from the university's public accounts from which they can pay for necessary expenses that do not fit into a state agency format.

Although the financial statements will show summaries of these foundation assets, the methods used to transfer funds from the foundation to support university activities will vary. Sometimes, the foundation will transfer money, and the university will spend it through its normal procedures. In other instances, the foundation will pay expenses directly, without going through the university accounting system.

Of particular note are faculty physician practice plans in universities with medical and other academic health center programs. These separate organizations in both public and private institutions hold the fees earned by faculty who participate in clinical medicine or provide other health-related services. The practice plans often hold significant fund balances, and the methods used to employ these funds on behalf of the institution vary. Like foundations, the practice plan may transfer funds to the university to use for institutional purposes, but the plan may also spend funds directly in support of other university purposes.

Further complicating this picture for public institutions, many state legislatures view any expenditure of funds for universities that do not flow through the bureaucratic processes of state government as suspect. In such hostile states, universities that operate effectively and efficiently with clear accounts run the risk of increased state interference. Ignorance and confusion are a form of protection in these environments. In many states, the legislature and other political actors may attempt to capture reserve funds that universities accumulate to support initiatives or sustain budget readjustments when required. Institutions often hide these funds in various foundation accounts or other places in their systems to protect them against expropriation by state agencies experiencing their own fiscal difficulties.

Nonetheless, good management for all institutions, public or private, requires an understanding of the university's finances. The key artifact for this is the global (or all-funds) budget that identifies the total sources and uses of money that supports the university's work. If a university understands where it earns its money and how it spends its money (all of it), then the institution can work to get the most academic value from the dollars spent.

Of particular importance to everyone engaged in higher education is an understanding of the major sources of funding for universities. Tuition and fees, state and federal financial aid, state subsidies, gifts and grants, sales of goods and services including auxiliary enterprises like housing and parking or athletics, research grants and contracts, intellectual property licenses or royalty fees, revenue from health care services or veterinary clinics, federal subsidies, income from endowment, other investment income, and annual giving all contribute money that makes the university's activities possible.

The structure of university finances varies. For example, some institutions have a higher proportion of tuition, endowment income, or state subsidy in their total funding than others. The structures vary not only among institutions but also by governance. Public and private universities, while they receive money from the same sources, receive their funding in different proportions by funding source.

In the constant effort to acquire more money for the improvement and expansion of the university's work, an understanding of the structure of university finance becomes critical. If tuition represents a small fraction of the university's funding compared to endowment income and annual giving, for example, then the university needs to focus on enhancing gift revenue, where the returns are the highest, rather than on expanding enrollment, which may have a lower return or even generate a loss when tuition and fees do not cover the cost of instruction.

## Public and Private Institutional Finance

If the state pays for enrollment by formula and increases funding as more students enroll or existing students take more credit hours, then enrollment growth may lead to increased income. This only succeeds if the amount the state pays for each new student or student credit hour plus whatever net tuition and fees the student pays is more than the marginal cost of delivering the additional instruction and maintaining the extra student. A university's decision about growing enrollment requires an understanding of the costs as well as the income associated with student credit hours.

Many elements determine the size of public universities, but one of them is the opportunity for the university to earn more from a state appropriation plus tuition and fees for each student than it costs to teach and maintain that student. Big is better under these conditions. With the declining portion of public university funding that now comes from appropriated tax-based funds and the increase in revenue from student tuition and fees, public universities increasingly focus on managing tuition and fee revenue and financial aid discounts rather than on simply increasing credit hours to benefit from a state funding scheme.

Private universities that cannot count on significant state appropriations per student may have a disincentive to grow. If the marginal cost of maintaining a new student exceeds the discounted tuition (tuition price less institutional financial aid) the student generates, then additional students do not create new revenue for the private institutions. The more an institution must pay through institutional financial aid (a discount from the nominal student tuition) to attract desirable students and subsidies from endowment earnings, the less revenue comes from increasing the student body. Tuition discounts are expensive, and if the institution cannot afford the discount, the quality of the student body will suffer. If the endowment subsidy declines, so too will the high quality of institutional performance, and if the high tuition paid reflects the consumer's belief that a college's small size adds value to education, increased growth may well deflate the institution's perceived value to its customers.

Public and private university finance often appear significantly different to outside observers, but in practice, the differences may not be so great. The private university looks to the earnings on its endowment to provide a stable income stream to support the costs of teaching and research beyond what net tuition payments provide, and the public university's reliance on state appropriations is really an endowment earnings equivalent. As a point of perspective, if a public university receives $300 million from state appropriations, this is equivalent to the earnings of an endowment of $6 billion (assuming a more or less standard endowment payout of 5 percent). Perhaps a dozen private universities have endowments at the $6-billion level. This helps explain why proposals to take public universities private fail, since replacing public funds with private endowment is usually an impractical proposition.

Although institutional size in terms of its undergraduate enrollment in both public and private institutions responds to many issues, the fundamental calculation turns on the relationship between the marginal cost of adding a new student and the net new income a student generates.

Universities with medical and other health-related schools or veterinary programs, or those that own or affiliate with hospitals or hospital networks, have another complex set of revenue opportunities and risks. Clinical faculty in medical, veterinary, and some other health profession schools can and often do produce a significant surplus from the revenue generated from fees for service that they hold in their practice plans. These funds are critical income to support faculty salaries as well as the costs of acquiring and performing work on federal and other research grants and contracts.

Hospitals, when well run, can generate revenue that supports the facilities and creates opportunities for the clinical faculty to practice and generate fees for service. The hospital can also support a variety of research activities or clinical drug trials that enhance the hospital's reputation and attract insured patients. However, the complexities of the clinical enterprise are significant, and the management of private payments, state or local subsidies, and federal medical reimbursement programs, in addition to liability and regulatory issues, create major challenges for large academic medical centers.

Many sources of university revenue prove unstable at various times. State universities continually struggle with the uncertain nature of tax-based funding, especially since the 2008 financial recession that saw dramatically reduced state income. The variations in state revenue can be substantial, in some cases resulting in reductions on the order of 10 to 20 percent in one year and perhaps continuing for several years. For public universities heavily dependent on state revenue, these reductions generate great financial stress. Responses include temporary or permanent expenditure reductions and substantial program reductions, and tuition and fees almost always increase. Although state funding for higher education often recovers after a decline, in recent years the recovery has usually been incomplete, producing a downward trend in public funding per student that appears likely to be a permanent condition in many states.

Some institutions find their flexibility to respond to rapid and significant reductions limited by obligations associated with debt service on new facilities, heavily tenured permanent faculty, strong union contracts, increasing health care and retirement expenses, and similar issues. Some responses are effective in the short term, such as unpaid furloughs of faculty and staff, but not for longer readjustments in financial structure. Public universities with relatively low tuition and fees compared to some of their public and almost certainly their private competitors can rapidly increase charges to compensate for reduced state funding. However, most students and parents, and many state legislatures, resist this tactic strongly. For some institutions, high prices may have an impact on enrollment.

Private universities have many of the same issues, although most are only marginally dependent on state contributions. The private institution will often find it difficult to respond to declines in revenue from endowment earnings, as their tuition and fee levels may already be near the top of the market.

Although these cyclical readjustments in financial resources affect all universities, those that are smaller, already have high tuition and fees, rely on those tuition and fees for as much as 85 percent of their operating budgets, and exist below the level of elite, highly selective institutions will suffer the most risk and forced change. Very selective public and private institutions and those with extensive resources in endowment and other institutional revenue may be able to weather these cycles without dramatic changes.

In every case, however, universities in today's highly variable financial marketplace find it increasingly necessary to build multi-year financial plans and create mechanisms to deal with a range of contingencies. No university has much difficulty coping with a windfall of funding. However, unless institutions budget ahead three to five years, they will continually find themselves improvising financial solutions and losing competitive position as a result.

## Chapter 9

# Budgets

------------------------------------------------

Money matters, as we have seen. Universities implement their values by how they spend their money. While many academics do not like to talk about money, preferring instead to talk about values, the basic structure of university life requires money to express values.

Academics speak often about values in the abstract. Much academic writing focuses on such issues, and many eloquent colleagues as well as critics write persuasively about the values that ought to prevail in academic life. Such commentary makes for stimulating and often inspiring reading, but when the warmth passes and it is time to do something to implement the values, almost everything is about money.

Universities disguise some of the conversation with study commissions that meet and talk about what the faculty, students, administrators, and others should do about curriculum reform, about student retention, about research promotion, or about undergraduate student life. Sometimes this talk results in an elaborate document outlining goals called a "strategic plan." The talk appears to be free, but it is not.

If faculty spend three hours a week for fifteen weeks on writing a strategic plan (which in most cases bears little relationship to the reality of money and performance), they spend time they might have used to develop a new course, apply for a grant, or write a paper. Work of this kind is only free if someone outside the university pays for the faculty hours spent in this activity. Perhaps talk is cheap, but it certainly is not free.

More important than the talk and its direct cost in lost work, however, is the budget. With a few exceptions, universities spend most of their income. When they manage to create a surplus, it normally ends up paying for deferred maintenance or being held in reserve for projects not yet fully funded. This circumstance of almost-full expenditure has a profound impact on the relationship of money and values.

Every university has a backlog of exceptionally valuable programs and ideas that it would like to implement but for which it has no money. Improvement of student life, introduction of technology, development of new academic fields, creation of interdisciplinary programs, expansion of international activities, engagement in community services, enhancement of research facilities, expansion of financial aid—the list is long.

For every new $100,000 available to a university from any source, the faculty, students, staff, alumni, friends, and supporters of the institution will have at least $1,000,000 worth of outstanding projects and probably at least another $1,000,000 of good but not quite as stellar proposals. Note that none of these qualifies as a worthless project, easy to dismiss. University people have no lack of imagination, creativity, or wisdom, and their good ideas overwhelm the funding capacity of every institution.

Each university decision about money is a decision about relative values. If we buy student activities and not research development, we have made a choice among competing values. If we choose to renovate old academic buildings rather than upgrade the football stadium, we make a value-based choice. If we choose to buy books for the library rather than increase faculty salaries, we make a choice based on our values. Each year, the university's budget serves as a snapshot of the values the institution chooses to support that year and has supported in previous years.

Some will say, "Oh, no, you have it wrong. The university cannot just choose to do something different with its money. It is constrained by this rule, that regulation, this contract, that state requirement." This is true to some extent but misses the point.

The values that the university's budget expresses do not necessarily reflect those of one individual or group, in one year, but rather the values the institution has acquired from all sources over the years. The snapshot of a single year's budget demonstrates those historical as well as current values, without assigning blame or credit to anyone in particular. It is simply a straightforward demonstration of the things that the university over the years has chosen to fund. For better or worse, those are the things that the university, its many constituencies, and its funding sources valued enough to buy. Those items not in the budget are things the university could have bought but did not.

The proof of this proposition is easily demonstrated. Whenever any group wants to change the university's behavior, it almost always does so by buying a different behavior through the budget. State legislatures, Congress, and federal agencies are among the most aggressive in this activity. If the legislature thinks there should be smaller classes, it will pass a law that changes the distribution of the budget to support small classes, or, if the institution is fortunate, it provides a supplemental appropriation to pay for the extra cost of the smaller classes. If it thinks the university raises tuition too frequently, it can deny authority to raise tuition. Federal agencies and Congress create incentives to invest institutional money in programs of interest to those entities. If a donor wants to see ethics taught at the university, he can provide an endowment in support of teaching ethics; if a corporation wants to see new business techniques researched at the university, it can provide a grant that pays for the research. The list is endless.

These examples demonstrate that external actors know they can affect the university's values by changing the budget. Yet the introduction of new activities funded with new money does not necessarily pose a major challenge to the university's values, even though it does affect them. When an external actor offers to buy something, the university does not subject the offer to a competitive test against all the other values the university might hold dear. Instead, it simply asks whether the new idea matches some element of the university's values, and if it does, it takes the money and implements the new idea. Negative adjustments come primarily from a loss of public funds or from declines in enrollment or endowment value, but these too reflect the values of external actors, whether legislators, governors, individual students and their parents, or active investors in the stock market.

Internal change in the allocation of money, however, gives a much clearer view of the university's fundamental values. No university actually constructs its budget from zero (even if the process carries the name zero-based budgeting). Instead, all university budgets result from incremental adjustments implemented over time. Probably at least 95 percent of a major university's budget supports the same activities every year.

Over many years, however, the 5 percent that does change shifts the institution's priorities. Over time, the money that no longer pays for the teaching of Latin and Greek pays for the teaching of computer science and environmental studies. This change represents a change in values: Computer science and environmental studies become more valuable to the university today than the study of Latin or Greek, subjects that were valuable yesterday. Every time the money buys something new or ceases to buy something old, the university's values have changed, and over time, the values can change a lot.

## Budget Systems

Because of the importance of budgets, universities experiment with many different systems for managing the budget. These often follow fads that have currency in public administration circles and perhaps the business world, and universities sometimes adopt these fads at about the time their effectiveness elsewhere has faded.

Zero-based budgeting, for example, had some currency a generation ago. This fad recommends that the institution build its budget every year from ground zero, questioning all expenditures in light of the organization's current values and opportunities. In practice, this is a labor-intensive process that results in marginal adjustments to the budget not much different from what would have taken place had zero-based budgeting not prevailed.

Like other fads, this one contained an insight. Institutions do need to understand their business from the ground up, and they do need to review their accepted priorities periodically. However, they do not have to pretend that everything every year is new.

### *Responsibility-Centered Management*

Another system with greater influence and effectiveness goes by the name responsibility-centered management (or RCM for short). RCM is another quasicorporate import. It recognizes that the organized units of the university generate both income and expenses. The key principle here is that if the university makes each significant unit within the institution responsible for earning its own income and controlling its own expenses, the university at large will be most efficient.

The budget system defines the responsibility centers (a department, a college, or an administrative service unit) and then creates the financial and bureaucratic infrastructure to assign income and costs to the centers. If a center spends more than it earns, it must reduce its expenditures or increase its income. If it earns more than it spends, it can reinvest the surplus in enhancing its unit.

This system has a beautiful simplicity and the appearance of tough, no-nonsense management. It appeals because it appears to put the authority for success into the hands of the local responsibility center managers. An additional advantage is that it appears to remove the conversation about values from the upper administration to the responsibility centers and perhaps to let the invisible hand of economic determinism and the market adjust the budget and, in the process, determine values.

A number of institutions embraced RCM in various forms and implemented parts of the system. RCM in its pure form, however, has had a difficult history for a number of reasons. The most important is that RCM makes some assumptions about the relationships between income and expenditure of the responsible units that may not apply to many institutions, particularly public universities.

RCM assumes that a unit has significant control over its income. In most colleges and universities in America, and especially in public institutions, colleges or departments rarely determine the price students pay for their courses, and state funding is delivered at the institutional rather than the unit level. University governing boards and sometimes external public agencies, or for public universities even the legislature, set standard charges for student tuition and fee income. As a result, the responsible unit does not control the price a student pays for the instruction delivered by the unit. The student generally pays the same course fee whether taking expensive courses in physics and music performance or inexpensive courses in Western civilization and art appreciation.

Although some universities do charge a premium for engineering and some allied health programs or admit students directly to colleges with differential tuition, the majority of undergraduates see a common rate for attendance. In practice, moreover, students do pay widely differing net prices as a result of financial-aid policies mostly unrelated to the financial structure of the units where they receive instruction or acquire a degree. As a result, a system that allocates income in terms of what students on average generate but expects the responsible unit to pay for the widely varying cost of the services provided cannot function as planned. Units with inexpensive instruction make subsidy profits; units with expensive instruction incur artificial losses.

Some universities, including those that implement versions of RCM, make technical adjustments to the average net tuition attributed to the earned income streams of various units depending on some understanding about relative costs, weighting the income from tuition and fees attributed to the physics department more than the income attributed to the history department. The process of determining these differential income attributions based on the cost of programs, however, creates a challenge of its own.

High-cost programs receive an income bonus in the tuition calculation that reflects the current expense of their program, not necessarily efficiency in its delivery. Inexpensive and perhaps more efficient programs receive an income deduction from the tuition calculation reflecting their current lower cost. These adjustments are complicated to calculate. The process of making such adjustments in a university can become a political conversation, and in that case, some of the benefits of the impartial market adjustment fade. Usually, however, universities use various national studies of program costs to attempt to set these adjustments at appropriate levels. Some institutions charge differential tuition by program or college, making such adjustments to a standard tuition and fee schedule unnecessary.

RCM budgeting also requires a system for allocating centralized costs. If each unit as a responsibility center pays all its direct costs and receives all its earned income, the university must allocate a proper share of the overhead costs of physical plant, parking, landscaping, heat, light, general administration, and other similar general expenses to each unit. One way to deal with these is to charge a standard overhead rate to all units (much as is done with grants and contracts). However, some units require much more overhead than others do. Laboratory sciences, for example, use many more common resources and much more expensive space than history departments. Most institutions also charge a tax to all the revenue-generating units to cover institutional initiatives, to finance special aid to transition units from deficit to balanced conditions, and, as is usually necessary, to support the deficits in intercollegiate athletics.

If, instead of a centrally allocated overhead cost, units pay directly for their own overhead for such common assets as building and plant, they may have a significant incentive to suboptimize. Rather than perform scheduled maintenance paid directly out of current revenue, they may choose to defer maintenance to increase current spendable revenue, leaving to the next generation of academic leaders the problem of funding the now-inescapable deferred maintenance.

Another challenge is the result of the core concept of RCM: The university will hold the units responsible for their financial behavior. This means that if the college of arts and sciences runs a deficit of $2 million, the university must insist that the college reduce its budget or increase its revenue by $2 million. In practice, most universities have found this form of accountability difficult to implement for both structural and political reasons.

In the arts and sciences case, if the cost overrun is the result of new facilities for which anticipated new revenue failed to appear, the requirement to pay debt service on the facilities makes budget adjustments in the college exceptionally difficult to achieve. Since most of the unit's expenses are in personnel, a sufficient reduction in current expenses may well prove impossible. Significant numbers of professors are tenured; others who are not tenured may be major revenue earners by teaching large classes or earning substantial grant or contract revenue. Any dismissals sufficient to adjust to a major budget issue would almost certainly require expensive due-process procedures.

As a result, the institution often subsidizes the deficit, the administrator responsible for the deficit in the unit returns to the faculty, and a new dean refuses to take over the operation unless the administration agrees to cover the deficit so the new leader can begin with a clean slate. This cycle, obviously, undermines the point of the exercise, for if the unit does not bear the cost of failing to meet its fiscal obligations, then RCM loses its benefit of enforcing responsibility and accountability. Universities can enforce fiscal discipline, nonetheless, but it requires strong leadership and central support. Good RCM implementations may well subsidize the new dean, but with a specific plan that will return the deficit unit to a balanced budget.

Equally of interest is the case of the college that succeeds dramatically, by virtue of a low cost structure or efficient and imaginative management. This unit will generate a large surplus, and it could choose to spend that surplus on enhanced salaries and improved amenities for faculty and students of the unit as well as other benefits. The other guild systems of the university may try to limit the permissible upside growth, arguing that such surpluses are really subsidy profits resulting from miscalculations of the RCM system. Limits on unit surpluses diminish the financial neutrality of the model. Worse yet, the central administration can sweep up surpluses saved for future use to cover other central responsibilities or initiatives.

RCM systems can also encourage other forms of suboptimization. Responsible units can all offer their own slightly different statistics courses when it would be more efficient for one unit to provide statistics instruction for students in all programs. If the revenue from credit hours sustains the responsible unit, then it will have an incentive to require as many credit hours as possible within the unit. Although the structure of the RCM implementation can constrain this behavior, it adds to the management complexity of administering the system.

Perhaps even more problematic, the RCM model does not offer direct incentives for quality but instead seeks primarily to maximize the positive result of the income-expense equation without necessarily requiring a consideration of quality. An effective university RCM system will need to include a quality-incentive element in addition to the fiscal accountability. Some institutions create a special tax on all units to support a quality-incentive fund, but to be successful it must reflect explicitly measured quality elements, not anticipated good news. University success requires money, but it requires money invested in improved quality as well as improved productivity, and it must know whether its investments actually do result in improvement.

In most universities, a final challenge of RCM comes from the complexity and sophistication of the data required to allocate costs and income accurately to the units. Many costs and much income of universities come from marketplaces managed and negotiated within the university, where competitive market behavior may have minimal impact. The more closely a university's income and expenses relate directly to the activities of the responsible units, the better RCM will work.

RCM has some significant insights. It recognizes that university efficiency and productivity are rarely top-down phenomena but instead work best when based on achievement driven by the units and academic guilds that do the university's work. RCM's responsibility centers focus on the people who generate the income, incur the costs, and produce the value. These people know best how to improve. It is also an excellent model for focusing attention on a careful analysis of income and expenses, a topic much neglected in academic administration.

## Performance Budgets

Drawing on the experiences of universities following RCM as well as the lessons of other budget models used in the past, universities today often have hybrid models that implement the best features of various systems. The most effective versions borrow from RCM to create what we might call performance budgeting, an approach that focuses on the improvement of productivity and quality. A number of principles adapted from various budget systems drive such an approach.

- Financial incentives work. Academics respond to the opportunity to earn financial incentives either for their units and guilds or for themselves.
- Global budgets and an accounting of all income and expenses are essential features of any effective budget system, and the institution must provide all the data collected to all the participants in the system in a clear, structured fashion to reduce the controversy that surrounds all university budget decisions.
- Good results come from tracking and rewarding performance on a relatively few key indicators. Great complexity in evaluation systems is usually not an advantage.
- The values that underlie the budget system must be explicit, recognized by the university units, and rewarded consistently.
- Good data that measure the productivity and quality of the institution and its units are essential.
- Academic budgets work best when they focus on improvement and provide rewards to units for specific, measurable results.

- Rewards must go to units for both productivity and quality improvement.
- Units must be held accountable for institutional priorities by meeting baseline expectations for productivity before receiving rewards for improvements in quality. These baseline levels of productivity must be explicit and accepted by both unit heads and upper-level administrators, and they must be visible to all university participants.
- Administration must take responsibility for articulating the values that the budget system rewards. Everyone must recognize that the values chosen for reward are the result of academic judgment and not mechanical or arbitrary reflections of a mindless financial system.
- The institution must operate a five-year budget plan that includes the most recently completed year, the current year, and a forecast of the next three years. Each year, the five-year budget rolls forward, adjusting the out years to reflect the actual experience of the just-concluded current year.
- Five-year budget plans force institutions to adjust their income and expense expectations to the realities of current and immediate past performance. Given the often inflexible nature of university commitments, the five-year window offers an opportunity to anticipate required changes.
- If successful, the performance budget system will generate significant internal opposition when initially implemented and will require at least five to seven years of consistent operation to become institutionalized. This is a challenge given the short tenure of many university chief executives.

*Mr. President,* says the senior dean on the dean's council, *this five-year all-funds budget we're working on is very difficult. We don't know what will happen in the future, and we deans think you're attempting something we can't do. Possibly,* says the president, *but you are making commitments today that will have to be paid over the next several years each time you hire a faculty member or recommend a tenure appointment, not to mention sign off on a research grant. Don't you think we should figure out what today's commitments mean for tomorrow? Well, maybe,* says the senior dean, *but you know that tomorrow I'll be retired, and you'll probably be at another institution. The new people will want to do something else, so why bother with all this? We've done OK working year by year. Ah, yes,* says the president, *if the budget follows your and my personal enthusiasms, the budget will surely change when the next people come on board. But the university is forever, and its budget should be stable and based on performance, not the personal charm and influence that you and I possess. Oh, Mr. President, I didn't know you were a Utopian,* laughs the senior dean.

For the purposes of an illustration, we can imagine a university that sees its future as dependent on success in delivering teaching and research. It may do other things, but the primary values it defines for itself are these two fundamental university purposes: teaching and research. An effective five-year budget for this example institution would focus on quality and productivity in the university's two primary products: teaching and research. The separation of these two elements of the university's work and the assignment of all costs and revenue (other than overhead) to these functions serve as key elements in the success of the model.

Equally important, however, is the development of a process for benchmarking quality and measuring quality improvement. Because quality evaluation is much less well-developed than productivity measurement, this activity takes much longer to propagate across the institution's various units than financial elements.

Finally, an effective budget system depends on the quality, consistency, and external validation of the measurements of quality and productivity that drive the budget. Measurement, for both productivity and quality, and a process for driving improvement constitute the core elements that allow an effective five-year budget system to support institutional success in a competitive marketplace.

*Chapter 10*

# Measurement

-------------------------------------------------------------

Universities collect data on a wide range of activities and functions. They count students, credit hours, faculty, and staff. They produce data on the budget with income and expenditures, the number of graduates, the number of admissions, and the number of applications. Universities can tell you graduation rates, persistence rates, part-time versus full-time students, number of fraternities and sororities, amount of sponsored research, grants received, grants applied for, and doctorates awarded.

Universities will provide data on athletic attendance and win-loss records, number of students employed after five years, starting salaries of graduates from the business school, and the number of alumni making donations. They know how many credit hours it takes to get each degree, the number and size of classrooms, and their utilization. They can report the number of small-, medium-, and large-enrollment courses. They have data on the availability of recreation opportunities and the ratio between instructional and research space. These are just a sample of the remarkable amount of information universities collect.

Universities provide reports to an extensive list of external agencies, although public universities report more data than private universities. These reports satisfy questions about crime on campus, ethnic diversity, athletic participation, and graduation rates of student athletes and non-student athletes. They respond to concerns about human subjects and animal rights, fraternities and sororities, scholarships or fellowships, other forms of financial aid, and overhead costs for research.

In every state, public universities respond to a mind-numbing series of special data requests to answer specific bureaucratic or political questions generated by state agencies, governors' offices, and legislators. Universities provide data to accreditation agencies, ranking organizations, disciplinary associations, and university lobbying groups in support of one or another agenda. The volume of this data is truly amazing.

While most universities have institutional research offices that manage significant parts of the data flood, many other offices of the university participate. The accountants generate accounting information, professional schools provide specific reports for their specialized accreditation agencies, athletic programs develop data sets for their conferences and the NCAA, the registrar produces student information, and the alumni association and fund-raising offices collect focused statistics on their constituencies.

A rigorous examination of all this data will produce despair. Each office produces data for the specific purpose intended, and different ones often use slightly different definitions, calculations, or data universes to deliver the results.

If we cross-check, to take one example, the data reported on annual giving and endowment to various agencies and reported in the university's official documents, we may get significantly different numbers. None of them is wrong, but each responds to the question differently. Do we mean cash in hand or include deferred gifts with their present value or their future value? Do we include premiums paid to purchase sports tickets and state matching dollars for private gifts? Do we include surplus university operating funds stored in the endowment fund? Are our reports on endowment as of June 30 or January 1? All of these variations and many others illustrate the peculiarities of university data.

Consistency for student information in complex universities is also difficult to achieve. Ask a registrar for the university's enrollment. There is no easy answer. Do we want fall, spring, summer, an average, or the total? Do we want fall enrollment on the first day or the fourteenth day of the semester, after drop and add, in the fifth week, by the fee payment deadline, or at the end of the semester? Do we want full-time, part-time, or headcount enrollment? Do we define full time as fifteen credit hours per semester or twelve credit hours per semester? Must we convert our data from quarter system to semester system?

Each university has its conventions for reporting these things, and the different agencies requesting the information have their requirements as well. As one might expect, the conventions differ from university to university and the requirements from agency to agency, rendering many comparisons based on these data difficult to interpret.

## Graduation Rates and Faculty Ratios

Even when we can agree on a definition, comparative interpretation may also prove difficult. Graduation rates are a favorite data point. Intuitively, people like this number, as it seems to tell them something about the efficiency of the university in educating undergraduate students. Graduation rates, unfortunately, have almost no validity as a comparative measure for different colleges and universities with any differences in student characteristics or academic programs.

If one university has 50 percent of its students studying part-time and another has 90 percent enrolled full-time, we can make no relevant comparisons of graduation rates since part- and full-time students have different paths to graduation and the official graduation rate statistic only measures the experience of first-time, full-time students. Student characteristics make a large difference in graduation rates that may not reflect the effectiveness of the institution. Wealthy full-time students who pay high tuition or have time-limited scholarships have high graduation rates compared to students in the same institutions who do not share these characteristics.

Many students today start at one institution and then transfer to a different institution that is closer to home, charges lower fees, or has more desirable programs. These students, even if in good academic standing when they leave, are usually counted as failures for graduation rates. The receiving institutions, whether acquiring the students from a community college or another four-year college, generally cannot count these new students in their graduation rate. When these transfer students receive their degrees, they do not appear in the statistics as successes because we calculate the graduation rate only on a base of the first-time, full-time, fall-enrolled students. When observers cite comparative graduation rates to make a point about college performance, well-informed people discount the argument.

Anything that divides by the number of faculty also usually produces a spurious comparative measure. Student-faculty ratios, for example, help institutions promote their campuses to the public. Many large research universities have numbers in the range of fifteen to eighteen students to each faculty member. Most small liberal arts colleges run from about eight to ten students to each faculty member. What do these numbers mean? Almost nothing. The student contexts of a liberal arts college and a large research university are much different.

Even among large research universities, the actual interaction between faculty and students is much less a function of some global statistic like a faculty-student ratio than it is of curricular organization, teaching mission, and the definition of what constitutes a faculty member. If faculty members include librarians, extension agents, and clinical faculty from the medical school, few of these faculty will have any impact at all on an undergraduate's opportunity to learn directly from a faculty member. Students in an honors program will have very different experiences from students in large-enrollment courses within the same university with the same overall student-faculty ratio.

Productivity measures that divide credit hours, research expenditures, or any other output quantity of the university by the number of faculty members are almost sure to deliver misleading results. One university may have four thousand faculty and another have three thousand faculty and produce the same amount of research funding. Is the larger university faculty less productive than the smaller one? Not necessarily, since the larger number of faculty may include primarily teaching faculty, extension agents, librarians, and clinical faculty who have no research assignment at all, while the smaller faculty may all be academic faculty with a research assignment and limited or no teaching responsibilities. The larger number of faculty may also teach many more students if its institution has a larger undergraduate population.

Finally, universities, especially major public and private research institutions, differ significantly in the structure of their curriculum and the number of disciplines they support. The existence of a medical school, a hospital, or a land-grant agricultural mission; an emphasis on arts and humanities or physical and natural sciences; the presence of an engineering college or a major business school; large numbers of contingent faculty—all these will affect data enough to render much comparative analyses of performance impossible.

None of this exempts the university from measuring what it does—quite the contrary. Universities must measure what they do if they want to improve, but they must collect and use data carefully to avoid misleading themselves.

## Data Audiences

University data have at least two quite distinct audiences. The first are the many external constituencies of the university, each of which may want to see data in different formats or for different purposes. In some cases, data in these contexts serve to defend the university against attacks, justify increases in funding, motivate alumni and friends, or in other ways tell a specific and targeted story. Whatever the external purpose of the data, universities should always recognize the special nature of such information.

The second and much more important audience for data is internal. These data should, in the best of all possible worlds, serve to drive the university's behavior, allocate rewards and incentives, and underlie the budget allocations that express the institution's values.

Universities often confuse these two different data universes. They will take data developed to defend a university against a legislative assault on its effectiveness and think that they represent a metric to drive the university's budget. Often this is inappropriate, not because the data are inaccurate (although they may be) but rather because the data express a reality in terms defined by the political context of a response to a legislative attack, not in terms related to the institution's need for improvement.

For example, if the legislature says that the faculty do not teach enough, a common complaint, the university will generate a blizzard of information on the role of the faculty in the classroom. This is fun, and it may confuse and distract the attackers, but data on the number of hours the faculty spend in the classroom, on the number of students who have interactions with faculty in groups of fewer than fifty, or similar topics often do not help the university actually improve the curriculum, enhance the student experience, or effectively use available faculty resources, although it may create good theater.

Universities will often seek out rankings that demonstrate how well they do, even when they know the rankings data are flawed, the methodology is unsound, and the results are unreliable. Because their constituencies have an insatiable hunger for evidence of institutional distinction, universities will promote and distribute rankings of dubious value simply to meet that need.

While reflecting the self-promoting enthusiasm of university leaders, the misuse of bad data becomes a problem if the institution believes its own propaganda and assumes it does well because its public relations office says so. It may be doing well, but not because a suspect ranking or television advertisement says so. Of course, there's utility in telling the world that someone else thinks you are doing well, even if that someone else is making it up.

The Institutional Research (IR) officer charged with providing data to the public finds himself, along with the PR officer, in a meeting in the president's office. She demands, *What is this table you want to release to the press?* The IR officer says, *It shows the change in research grants over the last five years. Yes,* says the president, *but it shows that we're losing ground.* The IR officer responds, *Yes, that's what the data show.* The president says, *You need to find a better measure than grants received, because we can't show a decline.* The IR officer thinks a bit and then says, *Well, we can show an increase in the number of grant applications we've made to the National Science Foundation. Will that do? Yes,* says the president, *that's good.* The IR officer leaves to prepare the table, and the president turns to the PR officer and asks, *What will the headline say?* The PR officer writes it out and gives it to the president: *University President Announces Growing Research Commitment: Research Grant Applications Rise as Faculty Compete with the Best in the Nation. Terrific,* says the president. *The trustees and alumni will love it.*

What then can a university do about measurement? The university can begin by recognizing that in developing comparative institutional indicators, a few measurements generally are better than many. A few measurements will serve this purpose well, and little improvement in evaluation comes from adding additional, more complicated measures.

For research, the total annual institutional expenditure on research from federal sources is one of the more reliable measures. The total annual institutional expenditure on research from all external sources that includes federal, state, local, corporate, and foundation research funding offers another good indication of the scale of the institution's research enterprise. The federal number is especially valuable as it reflects the competitive strength of institutions in the peer-reviewed marketplace of federal research grants. The *Top American Research Universities* publication includes these two items among its indicators of research university performance.

If the university wants to improve its performance, it must measure itself in a consistent fashion using a few key indicators and then track improvement. There is no substitute for this process, for unless the university has a reliable and consistent way of measuring its own performance, it cannot measure improvement. If it cannot measure improvement, it cannot reward it. Absent rewards based on clear and consistent measurement, improvement will happen in an idiosyncratic fashion if at all.

## Internal Data Audiences

University internal measurement falls into two general categories: the global indicators of performance and the operational measures of effectiveness. These are not the same type of measurement.

- Global indicators of performance serve to tell the institution and its units whether they are improving on the key variables that express the university's values.

- Operational measures of effectiveness help managers improve the operation of the institution so that the global indicators of performance will get better.

These distinctions are reminiscent of business indicators that provide the firm's board and investors with a few comparative global indicators of performance, such as stock price, price-to-earnings ratio, market share, and similar figures.

Operational indicators, however, help managers track sales targets, cost per unit of production, turnover time of inventory, cost of credit, efficiency of production, and similar process variables that contribute to the global measures of a firm's success. Boards and investors may look at only a few global comparative indexes to track the firm's success. They not only want the stock price to rise but also want it to rise faster than the stock price of similar firms in the market. They want to know the market share of their company, and they want to know the performance of their company relative to others in the same business.

Again, exactly how the firm succeeds in delivering good results is an operational issue for internal management. The results visible through improvement in the global indicators demonstrate the firm's success. It is management's job to get the results, and different managers with different circumstances will use different techniques to achieve good results. What count, however, are the results.

Universities, like large-scale business enterprises, have operational units with much different characteristics. An international company may make tractors, motorcycles, trucks, cars, and construction equipment, and each division will use different measures of productivity and quality to track its performance. University departments of chemistry and English, colleges of engineering and education, or divisions of health sciences and fine arts have much different operational models, definitions of achievement within a national context, and measures of operational effectiveness.

For universities, the results measures are the global indicators of performance, and the operational measures are what unit managers (the guild masters) such as deans and department chairs use to ensure that they are delivering good results.

An effective budget process as described above might well begin by dividing the university's products into the two categories of teaching and research. The budget defines the responsible units for this teaching and research as the schools and colleges of the university. It makes no assumptions about the responsible units beneath the level of the school or college, leaving this operational domain of departments and programs to the management of the responsible unit administration.

Having defined these two products—teaching and research—the university then creates a method for separately measuring the productivity and the quality of each product. Through its budgeting system, the university also develops a cost-allocation process that assigns all direct and indirect costs of the colleges to either teaching or research.

This important simplification serves to highlight institutional values. It asks the question: "what is most important for this university?" The answer in this case is "teaching and research," although universities could choose different values. In this example, we then must ask how to classify the indirect costs of academic advising, community service, and the host of other things that universities do. The measurement system that drives the budget answers this question through the following analysis.

The university's values actually exist in a hierarchy. Teaching and research exist at the top hierarchy of the university's values because without both, the university cannot succeed in its mission. Recognizing this hierarchy, the university assigns other costs to either teaching or research.

- Academic advising is a cost of doing teaching well, for example, so we charge its cost to teaching.

- Research and graduate program administration, for another example, are costs of doing research, so we charge their costs to research.

By putting all costs into either research or teaching, the university gains a clear means of evaluating how it invests its resources to accomplish its mission and, in so doing, makes explicit its values. Institutions assign the overhead for general administration (often including intercollegiate athletics) proportionally to the teaching and research budgets.

If, for example, an institution has an opportunity to participate in a community service project that will take three faculty members two weeks of work, the budget system recognizes that this effort represents a cost to either teaching or research or both. The community service may well be a good thing to do, but it will cost the university to do it.

By allocating the costs of projects, programs, and activities to either teaching or research, the system forces everyone to make clear choices and recognize that faculty work and time are valuable and limited goods.

If the university assigns faculty to do teaching and research, then when it chooses to reassign the faculty members to work on other projects it must, unless the faculty member chooses to work for free (an unlikely alternative in most cases), reduce the faculty member's commitment to the first two assignments. This makes the cost of teaching or research higher because the faculty member no longer works 100 percent on teaching and research, but the institution pays full-time compensation. Absent a special payment for the faculty member's time spent on other activities, the cost of the faculty member still falls on teaching and research, but without the full commitment of effort to those tasks. Again, it is not necessarily a bad thing to reallocate faculty time and effort away from teaching to support administration or service; it is just not a free thing.

Many academic people and their constituents dislike this conversation because it seems to deny the social or service missions of the university. This explicit recognition of the value of faculty work actually supports these missions because it requires all participants to be clear about what they want and what it costs.

Do they want the faculty working full time on teaching, on research, on public service, on administration, or on some combination? The problem arises when the university, in response to a call for public service or the desire to have more detailed administrative controls, diverts faculty effort to these purposes and then discovers that others in its constituency think the faculty do not teach enough or produce sufficient research.

When the institution's values and measures are unclear, universities find themselves attempting to meet everyone's requests without regard to resources. The result, naturally, is that more is expected of the university than it can possibly deliver, leading to an undeserved sense that the university is not an effective organization.

Actually, the university may be effective but unclear about the use of its limited resources. Universities that seek to please by accepting new obligations without making explicit the cost of these new obligations may be popular among some constituencies in the short term, but their overcommitment of resources will eventually diminish their effectiveness in their primary missions.

## Teaching, Research, and the Budget

Following through on our simplified example, to implement an effective budget process, the university must measure teaching and research.

Teaching has many forms and structures in a university, and measuring the productivity and quality of teaching poses some interesting challenges. Academics can imagine resolving some of these by designing unique and specifically tailored data systems to capture every nuance of the teaching process.

While such projects offer interesting and important intellectual insights, they usually do not provide practical measurement tools. Instead, universities often find they can get close enough to the issue of productivity using whatever accounting mechanism already exists for tracking course work for other purposes, such as assigning workload or certifying completion of degree requirements.

In most universities, credit hours are the common currency for instruction. Students define their progress toward a degree by credit hours; the faculty define their teaching work in credit hours; students and parents pay for credit hours; states often distribute money based on credit hours; and the faculty and accreditation agencies approve curricula in terms of credit hours.

For these reasons, most universities have good credit-hour data, and they can provide almost any information needed about credit hours. They can show how many credit hours students take on the way to graduation, calculate how many each faculty member teaches, or report how many each department produces.

An effective budget process measures its teaching productivity by credit hours and assigns the credit hours to the college that pays for the faculty time required to deliver those credit hours. The key here is to assign the productivity to the same unit that bears the cost. If a history professor teaches an education class, the credit hours belong to history unless the college of education chooses to pay the history department for the work of its professor.

The budget must also account for the differential productivity of large and small classes and perhaps the differential cost of high-investment classes in the sciences and lower-investment classes in the humanities. In practice, however, while elaborate weighting systems give comfort to those who think fine distinctions important, they actually make little difference in the results when dealing with complex colleges. At the department level, differential weights by type and intensity of class might make a difference, but in the scale used for college budgeting, the only productivity weighting that appears helpful is by class size.

This weighting, like all such systems, reflects a judgment, an academic value. The academic value is that the university should not provide financial incentives for large or small classes but should structure the system so that decisions on class size primarily reflect pedagogical issues rather than fiscal issues. To do that, the performance model assigns a higher weight to small classes than to large ones. The size of the weight is pragmatic, determined by an analysis of existing data to identify what weighting would produce the closest balance between large and small classes in the measurement of improvement.

The goal is to make small classes worthwhile, but not enough that a college could succeed in improving its productivity measure dramatically by reallocating all its faculty effort to small classes, a strategy that would produce low overall productivity. Similarly, the goal is to make large classes worthwhile, but not enough that a strategy of assigning most faculty effort to large classes would be more advantageous than a strategy that mixes large and small classes for reasons of pedagogy.

Almost all weighting systems of this type are based on the status quo. That is, we create a weighting that reflects the current structure of large and small classes. Then, the goal is to improve effectiveness and quality by improving the current system. If we have the balance right, departments and colleges will balance large and small classes to achieve an optimum that is better than current practice (more small classes if they have too many large ones, more large classes if they have too many small ones).

In practice, when installing an effective budgeting system, some departments and colleges will attempt to game the system. If the measurements used in the budget are carefully designed using good, current data, the weights will be such that the university can demonstrate that an overemphasis on one or another class size will not produce optimal productivity or give an advantage in earning the associated rewards for improvement.

> The business school dean storms in, irate. He tells the provost, *I've got the highest productivity in the university with my hybrid Internet-live instructor class system, and you want to reward units with small classes like violin performance. I'll kill the big class and only do small classes so I can win your silly productivity game.* The provost, no stranger to academic gamesmanship, says, *You haven't done the math. We weight large and small classes differently in the productivity formula. If you do all small classes, your school will lose, and if you do all large classes, your school will lose. You win when you keep your high-productivity large class and increase the number of small upper-division classes.* Yeah, maybe, the dean says, irritated that the provost did the math and he didn't, *but if that's true, how come the music school dean supports your plan?* The provost says, *She did the math and knows that her large music and art appreciation classes balance her individual instruction in violin and the small classes in music theory. Oh,* says the business dean. *I'll go recalculate.*

Research is the other top-level activity of the university. The measure of research productivity is much more complex than the measure of teaching productivity because no easy data element captures most faculty research in the same way credit hours capture most of the university's teaching. Nonetheless, for the university at large and for the colleges or schools within an institution, the total expenditures on sponsored research serve as a good surrogate. These data are available, and unit managers understand them well. Some units will have much greater opportunities and achievements in research funding than others, but the budget-measurement process resolves this problem, as described below. Sponsored research expenditures serve quite effectively for identifying research productivity.

The budget also tracks *fund raising* and *other income* at the top level of productivity evaluation. Both indicators measure success in acquiring funds other than those generated for sponsored research or teaching (principally state and tuition revenue), which were both accounted for previously, in support of the university's missions.

*Fund raising* refers to the development or advancement activities that solicit private gifts from individuals, corporations, or foundations on behalf of the university's missions.

*Other income* addresses sources such as clinical revenue, patent and license income, and some other forms of sales or service revenue.

As is the case with all explicit measures, these reflect and make visible institutional priorities. The institution recognizes that its opportunities for improvement depend heavily on the expansion of income sources in addition to research funding, state allocations, endowment income, or tuition support. For that reason, and to generate the incentives necessary for this effort, the institution includes fund raising and other income improvement among its top indicators.

In identifying good measures, a common concern has to do with scale and opportunity. When universities establish any standardized measures, the various guilds and their colleges immediately attack the measures as inappropriate or unfair for their particular guild. If the productivity number is credit hours, small units teaching foreign-language courses in small classes will feel disadvantaged in comparison to business schools teaching many students through distance-education methods. In systems that compare the total productivity of colleges and other units and reward those that have the largest share, these complaints have value. A good measurement system addresses this issue.

The university makes the academic judgment that each college is valuable for its specific contribution to the institution's programs. If the university chooses to eliminate a college or establish a new program, the measurement system for improvement is not the mechanism to accomplish a major redefinition of mission. Significant realignment of institutional mission or priorities, which includes both the addition and the elimination of programs or activities, belongs in special strategic reviews in response to opportunities or fiscal crises.

The function of good measurements is improvement in the university's existing programs, not program invention or termination. Within that context, then, the university uses the budget to create incentives for individual college improvement until each college reaches the highest possible level of performance. Few units ever reach the highest level of performance, but those which do need to improve to stay at the top against the competition, and the budget rewards the maintenance of top-level performance.

Productivity data serve to measure each college's improvement against its own previous performance. Within this measurement system, the university does not care whether architecture has as many credit hours as business. What matters is whether architecture has improved this year's performance against last year's and whether business has improved measured against the prior year.

Every unit can get better and receive a reward. Not every unit does, of course. The data serve to measure each college's or school's improvement against its previous performance. If a college gets better, it is deserving of a reward.

The same principles apply to research productivity. A research-intensive college of medicine should have high research productivity because such colleges are major players in the federally funded life sciences research marketplace. Colleges of fine arts, however, will have small research productivity measured in grants because the market for this activity in the fine arts is small.

Nonetheless, if a fine arts program improves from a $500,000 externally funded grant portfolio to $1,000,000 by virtue of successful application for grants and foundation funding, it will be more deserving of a reward than the college of medicine that remains stagnant at $20 million of research funding when comparable colleges around the country may well earn twice that amount.

These measures succeed because the focus is on improvement within the national context of the college, not in comparison to quite different colleges. If each of the colleges within the university improves within its context, the university at large will also improve. The aggregate performance of the university comes from the locally driven performance of the colleges. The budget must reward this college-based performance.

This part of the conversation about measurement focuses on productivity, for productivity is half of the measurement equation. Productivity measurement ensures that the colleges and the university get the most from the money available. Money, as all university people know, is required for quality and effectiveness. Money buys the people, the support, and the other materials needed to do academic work. The more money the university has, the more it can do.

Productivity improvement is equivalent to new money. Productivity improvement means doing the same work for less money or more work for the same money. Every dollar generated by increased productivity offers an opportunity to invest in quality, initiate new programs, or support faculty and student projects. Among the various sources of new money to enhance university functions, productivity increase is one of the few that is almost completely under the control of the institution and its colleges.

However, productivity alone does not suffice for driving an effective performance-based budget. Quality is equally important, for productivity without quality produces a poor result. If the incentive is for productivity alone, universities will drive quality down to the lowest acceptable level because no reward attaches to its improvement. Also, quality is harder than productivity. Faculty can easily add students to a class without increasing their own workloads by much, but increasing quality takes time, effort, thought, and work.

For this reason, the university must reward improvement in quality at least at the same level as improvement in productivity. Once a unit meets its baseline performance criteria, which demonstrate that it contributes teaching at a level required by the students and curriculum, improvements in quality or productivity produce separate rewards. Improvement in both produces a double reward.

Often, it turns out, the college finds that by improving productivity, it also improves quality because by being more efficient and effective it also does its work better for students and for research. As colleges improve, the budget provides dollar rewards the college can use to reinvest in additional quality for their units.

The performance budgeting as described here owes much to the insights of RCM by focusing attention and measurement on the work of the primary units of the university, usually the college or its equivalent. It attempts to capture both the productivity of the unit and its revenue-generating capacity, and it addresses the twin drivers of productivity and quality.

However, it is important to remember that these kinds of budget systems serve to drive improvement of existing enterprises, not to produce dramatic change in structure or mission. Because most university improvement is done through sustained incremental change, the more stable and predictable the measurement process that drives the budget, the more sustained the university's improvement will be.

*Chapter 11*

# Quality

------------------------------------------------------------

Quality is among the most elusive of academic measurements. Everyone speaks about it, everyone is in favor of it, and most academics believe they know it when they see it. But when we ask for specific measures of quality for departments, colleges, and universities, the task immediately becomes remarkably complex.

The *Top American Research Universities* publication groups research universities into clusters defined by nine indicators of quality. For the purposes of identifying clusters of high-quality research university campuses, this methodology serves admirably, even if it is not without controversy. However, the measurement of quality within the university at high enough levels of specificity and reliability to drive an effective budget process poses an additional challenge.

Budgeting to drive improvements in quality requires reasonably robust measures if it is to allocate dollar rewards effectively. Unless the university can measure something, it cannot reward its improvement. Incentives and the behaviors they generate require clear measurement.

## Quality: The Main Event

Although quality and productivity receive equal treatment in measurements for the budget, they do not play the same role in institutional improvement. Quality is the main event because the best universities are quality engines acquiring the highest-quality students, faculty, and educational and research programs.

Quality is an end in itself. In theory, perhaps, if an institution had one faculty member and one student, both of the highest quality in the world, it could be satisfied. This is the theory of extremes that drives sports and other winner-take-all enterprises. In universities, however, this approach is not effective. Universities do not have seasons, and they do not win championships for their academic performance.

Universities serve as stable, permanent, and continuing generators of knowledge, learning, and associated services and benefits to society. What matters to universities is sustained high performance in both productivity and quality. This is why we call universities quality engines.

Productivity speaks to the university's commitment to deliver a substantial volume of goods and services in exchange for investment by individuals, state and federal governments, and other support groups. Quality speaks to the university's commitment to deliver products and services that are nationally and internationally competitive.

The institution's success as an enterprise comes from its ability to compete in the marketplace for a substantial share of quality. Quality is scarce, and the competition for it intense. The relationship between productivity and quality often escapes academic observers, primarily because they underestimate the importance of both productivity and quality in acquiring the money needed to excel within the national and international quality marketplace.

## Context for Measuring Quality

Performance budgeting approaches quality from two perspectives: national and internal. Quality for research universities must be measured in a national context. Quality is not an abstraction but a specific measurement against a national standard. Each guild has its own national standards of quality, and what counts as quality for one guild may well be irrelevant for another.

To take a simple example, historians look to books and book-length monographs as the primary quality products they evaluate. Journal articles are significant, but they do not substitute for books. In scientific fields, however, the journal article is the primary vehicle for demonstrating research quality. In some fields, single-author publications determine quality, where in others multiple author publications are the norm. Science fields measure grants, while fine arts, theater, and music look to exhibits and performances. The variations on the definitions of quality multiply along with the expansion of fields and subfields within each guild and its subdisciplines.

Although measuring the quality of this complex mix of academic products may appear hopeless, university people are quite good at evaluating the quality of their colleagues' work in the same fields in other institutions. They tend not to explain the process to outsiders clearly, but they know how to measure quality, and if pushed, they can be explicit in the evaluation procedure.

If a university adopts performance budgeting and if it provides significant rewards for demonstrated quality improvement, the faculty will develop effective quality measurement. The measurement will not be perfect, of course, but it will be close enough to provide a fair basis for distributing rewards. Experience demonstrates that quality measurement requires two dimensions: an external benchmark relative to the national competition and a local measurement of improvement.

## National Benchmarking of Research

Ideally, all quality measurement would involve national benchmarking. In a national benchmark, the university measures the performance of an academic program relative to the best of its type in the nation.

Some think the goal is to measure against a peer group defined to be similar to their own institution, but that provides an unsatisfactory benchmark for universities that compete in the national marketplace for top faculty talent. Peer benchmarking tends to produce comparisons against carefully selected but relatively easy targets, making the unit in question look artificially better. Instead, universities must insist on national benchmarking against standards that reach into the top levels of performance.

Benchmarking for many disciplines is an expensive and time-consuming process. Most colleges, and their programs and departments, know what defines quality in their fields (number of publications, number of grants, type of awards, number of citations), but the data for a benchmark on these elements only sometimes exist in easily acquired, consistent, and comparative frameworks.

In many cases, colleges and departments have to assemble the data in a consistent form from their counterparts to demonstrate their relative national quality. The cost and time involved in this means that the units cannot accomplish the project every year. A three-year cycle for national benchmarking is probably about as much as it is reasonable to expect.

While the benchmarks set national levels of performance, they do not drive a performance budget effectively because they lag behind actual performance changes by the time required to collect the measurements (anywhere from one to three years). Budgeting is an annual, incremental incentive system, and its effectiveness depends on a short cycle between performance change and the delivery of incentive rewards. A solution to this problem is the addition of internal measures of quality improvement.

## Internal Measurement of Research

Internal measures of quality take the same measures identified for the national benchmarking and track an individual unit's performance from year to year, identifying and rewarding improvements as they occur. This provides immediate feedback and reward for improvement, enhancing the usefulness of the incentives. In addition, the internal measures can often be more detailed and more finely tuned than external benchmarks.

Even though this process appears relatively straightforward, it is not. Many colleges and departments simply do not want to participate in a program that makes explicit comparisons of quality. Many academics prefer to speak about quality in the abstract rather than measure it explicitly, either because they worry that their self-image may not match a data-driven evaluation of quality or because they do not believe in the performance-based budgeting process itself and judge that the best attack against it is to deny that it can support quality improvement. Whatever the motivation, two common errors often appear in the development of quality measures for colleges and schools.

*Mistaking resources for quality*: In this error, the unit will equate quality with the average salaries of faculty, with the number of faculty in the department, or with the size of the library collection in their field. These are important issues, but they do not speak to quality; they speak to the resources available in support of quality. If we say the university underpays the faculty, which may well be true, that says nothing about the quality of the work that these underpaid faculty do.

It is possible for underpaid faculty to produce high quality just as it is possible for overpaid faculty to produce low quality. The issue for performance budgeting is the quality produced. The performance measurement does not tell the unit how to produce quality; instead, it measures and rewards the actual annual improvement in the quality.

*Asserting that no measurable element of quality exists*: In this error, the unit will indicate that the work done by the faculty is so esoteric or indefinable that it cannot be measured in the specific way required by performance budgeting. In every case identified, this proves on closer examination to be false. The reason is simple. If there is no consensus in a guild about what defines high quality, there is no reason for the university to spend scarce resources in pursuit of what the guild cannot reliably measure.

In practice, every university guild knows what defines quality. Take, for example, the fine arts. Some will say that the quality of a musical performance, a sculpture, or a ballet defies a comparative measure of quality. Perhaps, but those who appreciate music, the visual arts, and ballet have a clear set of criteria for determining excellence: a review in the *New York Times*, shows at the Metropolitan Museum of Art, performances at the Lincoln Center, awards from nationally renowned piano competitions, and similar public reviews.

The elements that define the marketplace for artistic quality are as specific as journal articles for scientists in prestigious refereed journals. Once a guild's members discover that the rewards for quality improvement require a reasonable and measurable definition of quality, they almost always find a way to develop the measures and use them for internal improvement and external benchmarking.

*This quality measurement system isn't fair,* says the fine arts dean. The provost looks puzzled. *Why not?* The fine arts dean waxes eloquent. *Art is subjective; its value is in the eye of the beholder. You can't quantify the quality of art. This quality measurement system of yours may work for science types, but it's not any good for art.* Bemused, the provost says, *Well, if the art faculty can't find any national measures of quality, we surely don't need to pay much for them. We'll just get anyone who can draw and hire them cheap.* This response makes the dean angry, as it's intended to do. She says, *Of course we know what's nationally good.* The provost says, *You mean an art show in New York at a major gallery is more significant than a display in my living room? You mean an international piano competition is more significant than a recital in our local library? You mean an art review in the* New Yorker *is more significant than a review in our college newspaper of a local exhibit?* The dean, recognizing she's lost this encounter, returns to the fine arts faculty and puts them to work developing national benchmark measures of quality.

In some fields, national guild associations collect data on the publication rates and other defined elements of quality relevant to the field. Where these measures exist, they can help units demonstrate improvement. In particular, the recent development of the Global Research Benchmarking System, a collaborative project sponsored by the United Nations University's International Institute for Software Technology and the Center for Measuring University Performance, offers an effective and useful way to benchmark performance in the science, technology, engineering, and mathematics (STEM) fields. In measuring the frequency and impact of primarily journal publications in most STEM fields and subfields, the GRBS provides a reasonably accurate reference for quality performance and introduces the possibility of international reference groups.

## Teaching Quality

Finally, we come to the thorny question of *teaching quality.* This element of quality evaluation offers the greatest challenge and has the least satisfactory resolution. Overall teaching quality is quite difficult to measure, partly because the range of quality in teaching at first-rank universities tends to be narrow: most teaching is good to very good. Additionally, there is an almost complete lack of national guild standards for defining teaching quality. What we have in teaching is a competency floor. The guilds worry quite a bit about ensuring that all members are acceptable, even proficient teachers, but they do not worry about defining outstanding teaching quality.

Teaching is a performance art as well as a learning experience. The student evaluations used in most universities in the country have almost no utility in defining teaching quality. These surveys generate data that on close inspection tell little about what the student learned in the course, although they often tell something about how much the student enjoyed the course, how wisely the student believes the instructor evaluated the student's performance, or whether the instructor is popular—all different issues.

Because student evaluations are most reliable in assessing student enjoyment, instructors can improve their teaching evaluations by improving the entertainment value of their performances, a practice that can, although not necessarily, result in significantly lowered expectations for student learning. The aggregate learning of students in a department or college, a presumed outcome of teaching, defies measurement, although some institutions offer tests of critical thinking and other devices designed to discover what students have learned beyond what the grades in their courses signify.

Because the effects of teaching on individual students' course work are so difficult to aggregate, many colleges and units focus on the progress of students who choose particular undergraduate majors in their units. Through tracking the success of students in finding jobs, passing licensing examinations, going to graduate school, and attaining similar postinstruction outcomes, some indicators of success appear that may well reflect learning.

Additionally, some units can speak with authority about the quality of their graduate programs in terms of the qualifications of the entering students (scores on the GRE and other entry tests such as the GMAT, MCAT, or LSAT). Although these are input measures to advanced study, they can serve as output measures from previous educational experiences. Other output measures are less easily identified. Units can speak about post-docs awarded in some fields, about the pass rates on professional association tests, and about other external references that speak to the marketability of graduates.

The range of possible measures here is relatively wide, but the reliability of the teaching quality indicators is poor, reflecting the national inability to specify the measurable characteristics of quality teaching. National indicators related to teaching almost always fail because, in addition to the elements mentioned here, most teaching is a local product with a limited national marketplace.

Teaching is also a collaborative enterprise that requires the active and engaged participation of teachers and students. Students who do not want to learn or who arrive without adequate preparation are difficult to teach. Teachers who are indifferent and uninspiring make it difficult for willing students to learn. Calibrating the combination of teacher and student contributions to teaching and learning achievement proves considerably more difficult than many articles in the popular press might lead us to believe.

Given the importance of teaching and the student learning that results, much innovation and effort goes into explorations of different methodologies for teaching and evaluating learning. New techniques of instruction, technology-enabled feedback to assess learning and identify individual student difficulties, and many other innovations that affect both the instructional process itself and the evaluation of student accomplishment offer promise of significant improvement. As the effectiveness of these initiatives becomes better established, the pressure to see them implemented throughout the instructional process will surely increase, leading, perhaps, to better evaluations of the teaching process.

## Student Life

Many observers identify student life, student activities, and other nonclassroom student interactions as critical elements of the learning provided by universities. Although considerable sympathy exists for this point of view, measures of quality and productivity for student life prove even more difficult to acquire than measures of academic classroom achievement.

Professionals in student personnel administration count participation rates, activities, and involvement, and they run surveys that attempt to identify the impacts of elements of the college experience. They have also developed professional certifications to document the expertise required by their fields. In some cases these measures serve the purposes of evaluating student life and can lead to substantial improvement in the student experience, but whether they contribute to academic learning is a question not easily answered. These indicators offer some hope for developing good measures for student services improvement, but for now, few good measures that would support a system of reward exist.

Partly this is because student-affairs activities are much like other social services that have an infinite demand for their expertise. Universities can always use more counselors, student advisors, student activities coordinators, specialty service providers, or recreation centers. Establish a student service office, and it creates its own clientele in a matter of days. At the same time, the incremental benefit to the university's missions of teaching and research from any additional investment in these services is difficult to establish. For this reason, most student service activities end up as part of the support structure, evaluated in terms similar to physical plant, security, or parking services rather than as part of the educational enterprise.

Additionally, few faculty, especially in large research universities, take an interest in this activity, and the guilds do not regard it as part of their primary concern. The measurement of the quality of student life and the design of a reward structure to support that performance remain unresolved questions.

Under performance budgeting, every incentive focuses in the same direction: the measurement of teaching and research performance in quality and productivity and the incentive of a reward for improvement. Because the incentives all focus in the same direction, over time, the quality of the measurements themselves improve as colleges and units focus on verifiable demonstrations of continuously advancing performance.

# Chapter 12

# Managing Improvement

------------------------------------------------

Once built, a performance model focused on improvement requires an implementation plan. Often, models of effective operation produce elegant documents and much data but fail to engage the difficult task of implementation. University administrative and budget decision systems, built up over years of incremental change, resist systematic overhaul, and university guilds often resist most forms of productivity and quality management.

## Improvement and Resistance to Change

External constraints also inhibit change. In most public universities, legislatures and policy boards have rules, regulations, budgetary policies, and accounting and reporting procedures that may conflict with the data elements and goals of a performance-driven management model. In these cases, the process of reconciling such differences often sinks the accountability process with barely a trace and at best adds an additional layer of resistance to change.

Private universities with more clearly defined missions and some history of self-sufficiency often adopt these practices more quickly, not only because of their institutional history but also because their goals and governance structures remain aligned.

Public universities have multiple versions of institutional goals, they have multiple and cross-cutting governance structures, and as a result, they find accountable change difficult. In most cases, the public system chooses a method of high visibility, multiple reports, conferences, and task forces, all accompanied by minimal action and less improvement.

The successful implementation of a performance process that creates incentives for improvement often requires public universities to operate in ways familiar to multinational corporations, which must also function in complex and inconsistent environments. The technique involves the maintenance of different reports for different purposes:

- On one side, the university meets all the requirements for reporting and accounting required by external constituencies, government agencies, governing boards, and the like.
- On the other side, the university manages its internal operations in accord with the reports required by its performance-based budget.

Multinationals often do essentially the same thing. They report their performance in formats that meet local government regulations, but they also maintain a set of consolidated company reports that permit them to drive the corporation's quality and productivity on a consistent worldwide basis.

Any effort in a public university to reconcile the external requirements of government agencies to the internal drivers of quality and productivity will almost surely derail the performance process, because the state's interest in the management of higher education almost never focuses on questions of high performance and national competition. Many states also have the traditional resistance of the civil service bureaucracy to incentives and rewards for performance, preferring instead to support across-the-board and formula-based resource distribution systems.

The most important element in the implementation of a performance-based model such as the one described here is a commitment to make it work. That means that the president or chancellor and provost must do what the method they have endorsed says they will do, and the governing board of trustees must support the effort.

When the performance system says that the university will reward productivity and quality according to a specific set of measures, then the institution must reward that performance. When the measures demonstrate a lack of productivity or quality, the university cannot then lose its nerve and make an exception by saying, "Oh, my goodness, we didn't expect that it would cause our favorite college to lose a reward."

At the same time, if the university is to be explicit in its allocation of rewards, it must also be prepared to demonstrate to all unit heads or deans where the productivity of their colleges failed to improve and why the quality data do not justify a reward. This permits a dean to challenge the data, although in most cases, in a well-run system, the productivity data are quite objective and the quality data come from sources already defined and approved by the college leadership and its faculty.

Some of the incremental adjustment in a unit's budget may well be negative, following a failure to meet quality or productivity expectations. The university can withhold funds to fill vacant positions, reduce support for unproductive research programs, or, perhaps most significantly, identify new leadership for an underperforming unit.

Most academic guild masters, such as deans and department chairs, have long experience with administrative innovation. They know that strong, if sometimes passive, resistance and various forms of delay can often end such initiatives before they enforce real performance accountability. Consequently, the institution must execute the model consistently over an extended number of years, make money follow the measurements, and demonstrate that the system works.

Some observers think it essential to revamp completely the budgetary operations of the institution to achieve change. This misunderstands the nature of the academic enterprise. Most of what universities do is done well and done right. The great bulk of the institution's business happens as it should. Change and innovation, improvement in quality and productivity, come at the margin of the enterprise as the result of consistent incremental change over time. A successful management model creates a financial margin and then moves that margin to support productivity and quality.

However, if the distribution of incentives and rewards follows political aims, personal networking, or other nonperformance criteria, the institution's people will do whatever the institution rewards. The power of the performance-based budget that follows explicit and visible criteria is that it makes political and personal relationships within the university much less valuable than the measurable academic performance of individuals and units.

Most university people, like almost everyone else, tend to do what the microsystems of which they are a part choose to reward. Over a relatively short period, if the university administers the budget plan clearly and effectively, the members of the institutional guilds will modify their behavior to compete for their share of the margin. The margin defines the improvement possible, because the continuing operation of the university requires the majority of institutional resources.

If a college wants to get better, it requires a few more faculty, not an entire new faculty. It needs a particular piece of laboratory equipment, not an entire replacement of all equipment. Spending at the margin changes institutional behavior. Improvement, not dramatic, revolutionary change, is the process required for institutional success. In time—a time measured in years, not decades—consistent pursuit of improvement at the margin will transform the university.

Some guild masters worry that the process of applying the results of performance budgeting may be either too mechanical or not mechanical enough. Performance budgets, like every other useful management model, are only tools for the application of academic judgment. The purpose of the budget structure is to make academic decisions consistent, reliable, explicit, and data based. It provides a demonstration of what the university expects, and it defines explicitly for all participants how the university will measure achievement.

It does not substitute for academic design, judgment, or values; it simply insists that the money allocated by the budget must match the values articulated by the university in a data-driven, consistent, and visible fashion. This is not a mechanical model, applicable to all institutions under all conditions, but a designed system that requires careful calibration to include the university's goals within the context created by the institution's circumstances, regulatory environment, and management authority. In addition to driving rewards on the margin, universities that seek to improve must also look at all of their systems and operations to find ways to enhance effectiveness.

## Improving Student Progress

Take, for example, the issue of undergraduate student progress toward degrees. In large, complex public universities, students have many choices: they can select among many majors, and they can change those majors. The choices are so numerous, however, that only some undergraduates have clear, focused, and continuing advice about how they should navigate through the university's rich but complex academic environment.

Colleges, departments, and faculty normally take responsibility for those students majoring in one of their programs, but many undergraduates do not commit to a major for a year or two while they take general education courses. The results of this system, if badly managed, appear in various places. The symptoms vary, but for the purposes of this discussion, we can review a particular case.

In this case, the symptoms of poor undergraduate management began with student dissatisfaction with the process of undergraduate education. In surveys, the students indicated satisfaction with the quality of teaching and dissatisfaction with anything that involved the bureaucracy of instruction (such as getting classes, understanding prerequisites, or finding good advising).

A symptom of this malaise appeared in the process of reviewing enrollment management. The university discovered a large backlog of demand for beginning laboratory and technical English courses. These courses, required for many students to graduate in various disciplines, appeared in too few sections each semester to fulfill student requirements, and many freshmen could not complete some basic courses until their junior or senior year, when they had earned sufficient priority to enroll in what should have been first-year courses.

Another symptom appeared in the drop/add process, where students, after an initial registration, decide to drop one course and add another. A high volume of drop/add transactions produced a form of course enrollment churning that caused delay and much frustration.

An additional symptom appeared in the form of the excess credit hours on a student's transcript that contributed nothing towards requirements for graduation. These excess hours reached a high average of twenty-four credit hours per graduating student, representing two extra semesters of full-time enrollment that contributed nothing towards the final degree. Other symptoms related to these were high dropout rates, low retention rates, and the consequent relatively low graduation rates.

In a university with over thirty thousand undergraduates, any confusion and lost motion in the educational process represents a large cost to the institution as well as to the students. The university recognized that managing this enrollment had become a necessity and proceeded to solve the problem through the introduction of a simple to describe but complicated to implement system called universal tracking.

Universal tracking took the classic notion of a collegiate four-year education and implemented it within the complex environment of a major land-grant, multi-disciplinary institution. It said to every student, *you must do these things:*

- Select a major on your first day at the university, or at least a general area for a major such as science, social science, math, business, or humanities.
- Stay on track toward that major every semester and select a specific major as soon as possible but no later than by the end of the fourth semester.
- Meet with an academic advisor if you fall off track during any semester by failing to take and pass a required course, and create a plan to get back on track.

In exchange, the *university promised every student the following things:*

- You can change your major any time you want, with the advice of a counselor.
- You can degree shop online at any time. Degree shopping online shows a student what would be required if that individual student switched to a different major: how many courses already taken would count toward the alternative degree, what additional prerequisites might apply, and how many additional courses would be needed to complete the new major. Online, students could browse through the hundreds of majors the university offers and test as many

interesting ones as they would like, with immediate and individualized response from the computer system.

- You will always be able to get a seat in a required course specified for your major track in the semester or year that you need it, but you must take the required course when the track for your major indicates, even if the available section falls in a less-desirable time slot.

This agreement between student and university is not all that different from the experience of students in small, private liberal arts colleges, although in those environments the management issues take place at a scale that is personal and individual rather than computer driven. After a considerable effort by faculty and computer designers, this system went into effect. Enrollment management improved dramatically, excess hours fell, retention and graduation rates rose, the number of students dropping and adding classes sank to an all-time low level, and student satisfaction with the academic bureaucratic processes rose.

The focus on these issues and the commitment to resolve them in a way that was student-centered had the interesting benefit of improving a wide range of other university activities. Colleges and programs found it necessary to specify clearly and carefully what they required for a major and at which point in a student's education specific prerequisites or other courses should be completed. Many departments and programs ended up revising and improving their curricula. With a clear understanding of all the students' expected majors and the courses needed to complete their degrees, the university could do a much better job of scheduling classes, with the result that fewer over- and underenrolled sections appeared.

The decline in drop/add is instructive. Previously many students participated in drop/add because they could not get required courses. If a student needed calculus but the course was full, she would sign up for English literature as a placeholder, hoping that during drop/add someone would give up a place in calculus and she could get in. She had to enroll in something to maintain her full-time status for financial aid and eligibility for many campus privileges (sports tickets, for example).

At the same time, another student who needed English literature found it full, and he registered for United States history as a placeholder. At drop/add, if our calculus student went in first, got her calculus class, and dropped the English literature class, then our literature student could pick up the literature class and drop the history class. However, if the literature student tried to use drop/add first, he was out of luck and had to keep trying to change into the desired course. Obviously, students saw this as a frustrating and inefficient system. Tracking eliminated most of this course churning through drop/add, leaving only legitimate course changes for this function. Equally positive results have taken place at other complex institutions that have implemented similar student tracking systems and developed more sophisticated versions.

The message here is that performance budgeting at the top level is not enough for improvement. The university must evaluate all of its systems all of the time in search of things that do not work well or that could work better. Multiple incremental improvements create greater productivity, reduce costs, and generate the margin that the institution uses to finance academic quality improvement and innovation.

The phone rings in the office of academic affairs, and on the other end is an agitated helicopter parent. *I want to talk to the person in charge,* he says. The experienced staff member transfers the call to the dean of students. *Good morning,* the dean says. *How can I help you?* With emphasis, the parent declaims, *You people can't give my child the courses she needs to graduate. She needs technical English, and there's no room in the course. You have to fix this or I'm calling my senator.* The dean, impervious to the irrationality of helicopter parents, asks, *What's your child's name and social security number?* The dean then says, *Just a minute. I'll get her records, and we'll address this immediately. Well, I hope so,* says the parent. The screen comes up with Suzy Jones's file. Thanks to universal tracking, the dean now has something to tell the parent. *OK,* he says, *I see that Suzy does need the technical English course this semester. I also see that we offered her a seat on Monday at eight a.m., and she rejected it. We then offered her a class on Wednesday at six p.m., and she rejected it. Then we provided her a chance to take it at two p.m. on Friday, and she rejected that too. So it appears that Suzy had three chances to take technical English this semester, and she chose none of them.* There is silence on the other end of the line. Then the helicopter parent says, softly, *Perhaps I'd better talk with Suzy.* The dean says, *Well, if she needs help, please have her call me.*

*Chapter 13*

# Support Services and Special Units

------------------------------------------------------------

L arge universities do many things in addition to teaching and research. Support services have greatly expanded as institutions of all sizes find it essential to serve the special needs of their students, faculty, and staff. Institutions have specialized offices to support international students and faculty, special-needs students, students with emotional, financial, or family problems, and other groups needing particular expertise. Some of these services respond to legislative mandates while others exist to ensure the widest possible access to the institution's resources and programs. However, several special units are of particular significance because of their sizes and impacts on the budget.

## Auxiliary Enterprises

Auxiliary enterprises provide relatively unsubsidized services to the campus community and other constituencies on a user-fee basis. These businesses include residence halls, campus centers, parking, food services, laundry services, and bookstores. They exist to help the university fulfill its mission but operate in a marketplace mode that requires them to recover their costs. Almost all represent services that private enterprise could and sometimes does provide under contract. Increasingly, universities seek ways to outsource some of these services where a private business can deliver the same functions more efficiently and less expensively.

In some instances, universities outsource because their customers want services the university cannot provide. A classic case in this instance is food services. Today, in many universities, students often prefer branded fast food to traditional university cafeteria fare. Universities discovered that students voted with their feet, spending more and more of their nutritional dollars at branded outlets off campus, such as McDonald's, Wendy's, or Taco Bell, rather than at university-sponsored generic food services.

To keep revenue and support student preferences, many universities contract with branded franchises to provide food services on campus in various ways. Universities frequently find it more effective to contract out all their food services, including enhanced traditional cafeterias or snack shops and general catering activities, to large-scale commercial providers who can sometimes do it better for less.

*Bookstores* are another example. What once was a unique service provided to the campus because community bookstores could not carry a full line of required instructional texts can now be provided more efficiently by large firms. Chain bookstores have outlets in every community, and these enterprises will provide every special service of the campus bookstore, usually at a discount.

Most universities recognized that they had little comparative advantage in this business and contracted with large chains to provide bookstore services on campus to serve students and faculty. Moreover, in today's marketplace, bookstores have more revenue generated from merchandise unrelated to the academic mission: logo apparel, backpacks, computer gear, and the like.

The book business for universities must respond to the same pressures as commercial book dealers, with Internet outlets such as Amazon.com providing highly competitive services at favorable prices.

These decisions reflect a market-based assessment of the university's ability to compete. If the university cannot compete on price or quality, then it should outsource. Other services that are usually outsourced are specialized maintenance of copiers, air conditioning, and elevators; some forms of computing; e-learning platforms; and in some institutions even general building housekeeping and maintenance.

Other functions do not lend themselves as well to outsourcing. For example, institutions that manage residence halls, a major auxiliary in most universities, often find that the demands of operating these specialized housing units for undergraduates require direct supervision. The expertise of student affairs personnel is necessary to manage student activities and support the academic work that may take place in these halls. Nonetheless, privately managed residence facilities for students, usually above the freshman level and especially for graduate students, continue to appear on campus or close by.

Other enterprises are more explicitly related to the teaching and research missions of the university. Five of these have special significance.

## Agriculture

Agriculture, for a land-grant university, represents one of the institution's signature products. By design, land-grant universities create programs and develop research in support of the agricultural industry of their states. Some part of what the agricultural enterprise does falls directly into the general university research and teaching mission, and the regular budget process evaluates and measures productivity and quality as it would for any other academic unit. Colleges of agriculture and veterinary medicine deliver degrees, teach courses, compete for grants, and in general operate like any other college.

At the same time, the agricultural enterprise also delivers research and extension products directly to the industries and individuals it serves. In most states, this university activity receives dollars directly from state government for the purpose of delivering research and extension, funds from private enterprise commodity groups, and a variety of support directly from federal or local county sources. Some also generate significant revenue from the sale of research products, such as disease-resistant or high-productivity crop varieties.

Separately funded units of this kind appear in the university budget much like a grant. The university expects the nonacademic agricultural activities supported by direct funding to produce a quality product for the agricultural industry of the state and other consumers. The university's obligation is to ensure that an agricultural program delivers this product efficiently and appropriately to the state or national constituencies that provide the funding, just as the institution ensures that other grants or contracts for research or services deliver expected results.

Agricultural research and extension appear as a special unit within the budget, and the accountability for their success is primarily external to the university rather than internal through that budget. The university ensures that the program runs well and that it is responsive to its constituencies. The institution also works hard to increase the funding for those activities, but the budget treats this enterprise as a self-supporting activity responding to external marketplaces and therefore not part of the regular reward-and-incentive structure applied to academic units.

Over the last several decades or so, the agricultural mission of the land-grant university has changed substantially. These units once provided general instruction on good agricultural techniques to family farmers, health and financial advice to farm families, and a variety of other support services oriented to the farming economy. Today's agricultural industry depends much less on individuals and more on corporate or large-scale private farming companies with extensive capital and management abilities of their own.

As a result, many of the functions that once were vital to the farm ecology have become much less so, and the constituency finds it harder to compete for the state dollars to support many traditional extension service activities. The major crop research programs that develop new varieties of standard products, such as corn, wheat, rice, sugar, and citrus, and livestock programs in some states, remain important, and the industries and the state will usually support these activities. This research creates value by increasing productivity, creating disease-resistant varieties, identifying better ways of managing pollution and water control, and other important topics.

The shift to focus on research and support of the major high-value crops and away from the individual support of farm families is often challenging to traditional land-grant programs and their supporters. In the reduced financial circumstances of many states, these programs have less of a claim on state dollars than other social programs delivered by other agencies.

## Clinical Medicine

A second large university enterprise is clinical medicine, which in some universities includes one or more teaching hospitals. In some instances, the university does not directly manage academic teaching hospitals; rather, they exist as affiliated but separate not-for-profit corporations with which the university maintains a variety of associations and contract-based relationships.

The clinical enterprise primarily involves the academic colleges of medicine but also includes the activities of dentistry, nursing, other health professions, pharmacy, and veterinary medicine. All of these colleges operate clinical services that provide care to patients and receive fees or reimbursements as a result. These fees go into practice plans, a form of external account that can receive and disburse funds in support of the colleges' activities. The practice plans pay the cost of providing the services and return the surplus to the colleges involved to subsidize teaching and research.

The test of success for these units lies in an external and often highly regulated and competitive marketplace for health care. Faculty physicians and other health care providers deliver these services and at the same time perform a variety of research and teaching functions. An elaborate system of external reviews regulates the quality of the service, and the university ensures that the financial operations remain positive.

Clinical medicine can be a major generator of support for the academic and especially research programs of colleges of medicine and other health sciences. Absent this subvention from the revenue generated by clinical activity, including the clinical trials used to test the development of new drugs and the revenue from licenses and patents of new medical treatments and devices, the research missions of these colleges would falter, decline, and in some cases disappear. Consequently, the university pays close attention to the business issues associated with clinical medicine. This does not directly affect the academic performance budget because clinical medicine operates in the external marketplace and is a self-supporting enterprise, not an activity within the university's direct academic mission.

University or university-affiliated hospitals constitute another major concern for institutions with significant medical school commitments. Some institutions manage their academically related hospitals directly as affiliated businesses, some have arm's-length relationships with their hospitals through a not-for-profit board with university membership, and others work with multiple independently governed hospitals through contract relationships.

The businesses of hospitals and clinical medicine performed by physicians follow somewhat different business models. For this reason, a clear separation between the financial operations of the academic and physician side and the hospital management side of the relationship is a critical element of a successful academic medical enterprise. Without that separation, usually captured through formal agreements and contracts, neither the hospital nor the medical college can know clearly whether it is operating at optimal effectiveness.

Academic medicine requires a strong hospital relationship (with one or many institutions), and hospitals benefit greatly from the participation of physicians, students, residents, and fellows in their work. Well managed, the relationship between academic medicine and affiliated hospitals is a benefit to both. The complexities of funding and reimbursement structures for hospitals and physicians and for academic medical training nonetheless require highly expert and effective management.

## Intercollegiate Athletics

Intercollegiate athletics are also of considerable significance in almost all public and private universities. This enterprise serves a host of functions for the university. In America, big-time intercollegiate sports have been a part of the invention of almost every major American comprehensive research university. Harvard, Yale, Princeton, Michigan, Berkeley, Stanford, Chicago, Illinois, Ohio State, Florida, and Texas, to mention but a few, all have grown and prospered at different times as major institutions within a context supported by big-time intercollegiate sports, especially football.

This relationship, in existence since the beginning of the twentieth century, originates as a consequence of the funding model for American higher education. Absent federal higher education policy, funding, or control, colleges and universities sought a mechanism to capture local and alumni support across the generations of graduates. Sports proved to be one of the effective mechanisms for accomplishing this.

Early in the twentieth century, American colleges discovered that intercollegiate sports competitions, especially football, could attract large audiences and sustain the interest and attention of alumni and donors. Organized competitions delivered repetitive annual athletic campaigns followed enthusiastically by university supporters, including many graduates from years past whose interest in sports kept their interest in the university vital. Throughout the early years of the twentieth century, public and private colleges developed a sophisticated system of intercollegiate sports management that continues to deliver high-profile, high-cost, and high-visibility products for the institutions.

One of the key elements in American college sports success has been the invention of a franchising system that regulates and standardizes college sports for all participants within the following context.

- During the first decade of the twentieth century, colleges and universities created an external private, not-for-profit membership organization and then agreed to delegate all significant aspects of college sports regulation to the association. This franchising organization, the NCAA, operates the franchise system on behalf of all member institutions.
- The NCAA establishes the criteria for college sports franchising by standardizing all aspects of college sports competition (rules of the game, rules defining the participants, rules defining the competitions).
- The NCAA then licenses a franchise back to the participating institutions to operate an intercollegiate sports program with the requirement that each institution must follow detailed, specific, and standardized franchise requirements.
- This system gave America's colleges and universities a standardized sports product even when the institutions themselves had greatly differing size, scope, wealth, student characteristics, governance, and other characteristics.

- Every football, basketball, or volleyball game, for example, played by two franchise institutions takes place with the same rules and under the same conditions, permitting intercollegiate games and championship competitions among institutions of differing types for many sports.
- The NCAA college sports franchise, while it mandates uniformity of sports rules and operations, leaves the branding of the sports teams and related activities up to the individual institutions. As a result, the colleges gained a large and effective marketplace to develop high-quality standardized sports competitions under their individualized institutional brands, thereby maintaining institutionally specific and dedicated constituencies for each college or university.

The top level of football, while it conforms to franchise requirements for the operation of the games and the treatment of student-athletes, controls a postseason competition through bowl games and a recently introduced four-team playoff system. The creation of these bowls reflected entrepreneurial activities of the private bowl venues that promoted the games to generate revenue for the bowl enterprise. The bowl enterprises engaged conferences and institutions in a variety of postseason competitions, which were heavily influenced by television network financing. Originally designed around traditional end-of-season games between the champions of paired conferences, the bowls evolved into high-stakes competitions involving large sums of money from advertising and television revenue. Because the bowl system does not actually run a championship like other NCAA sports, the pressure to create a playoff system became irresistible. The long discussion of variations on the bowl system to approximate a championship have produced a four-team playoff plan beginning in 2014 that will produce a champion and significantly enhanced television revenue. Whether this method will prove satisfactory remains to be seen.

Although remarkably successful, this franchising system generates a number of problems, mostly resulting from its success. By creating a standardized competitive environment for sports competition for institutions of every size and level of resources, it also creates an imperative for institutions to try to invest equivalent amounts in the standardized competition. Institutions with limited resources find it necessary to compete against institutions with much more money because all institutions play the same games by the same rules. Everyone's alumni and supporters want to see their alma mater perform well against the national competition.

Sports, of course, are unambiguous activities designed to produce clear winners. Winning is the purpose of the exercise, and within the standardized franchise system of the NCAA, institutions compete intensely to acquire the talent essential to winning teams. Further, the franchise system established by university leaders in the first half of the twentieth century included the concept of "program." A program is a collection of sports, not just a single sport such as football. The franchise requires participating institutions to deliver a program with a specified number of standardized sports competitions. No institution can concentrate on football to the exclusion of track-and-field, for example.

This requirement to maintain a program has the benefit of ensuring that franchise participants will all have sports activities that involve many students with a wide range of athletic abilities and interests, thereby keeping sports closer to the academic enterprise. The requirement also has the less-desirable consequence of requiring substantial investments in the operation of multiple sports teams within intercollegiate athletic programs at all participating franchise institutions.

Over time, the history of college sports has demonstrated the success and challenges of this franchise system. While successfully defending the franchise operation against many threats, some resulting from corruption associated with competition in the recruitment and retention of athletically talented student-athletes, the franchise system's success created some significant distortions of university resources that today represent a special challenge for university management.

The participants at the top level of intercollegiate sports franchises operate on budgets of around $100 million or more a year. This is about the range of a significant academic school or college. All but a few of the most successful college sports programs lose money. They charge admission for popular sports such as football or basketball, collect revenue from concessions, earn payments for sponsorships, television appearances, and advertising, charge students special athletic fees, assess fees for luxury seating in stadiums and ballparks, seek donations, and acquire other income from a variety of sources. Even so, each year almost all college sports programs cost more to produce than they earn from the revenue they generate. The institutions absorb this cost into their operating budgets in much the same way a corporation absorbs advertising and public relations expenses.

Long-term success for an intercollegiate sports franchise requires three things: high-quality and relatively scandal-free management, a winning tradition, and a financially solvent budget. This is the university's responsibility. However, these programs usually operate much like auxiliary enterprises, even though they may lose money and require a subsidy from the institution's general funds. As extracurricular enterprises, they do not participate in the university's academic performance budgeting.

In almost all colleges and universities, no matter what the size, the institution's general budget must fund the athletics deficit. These subsidies for intercollegiate sports represent a direct cost to teaching and research, even if they are located elsewhere in the institutional budget. As with the advertising and public relations mentioned above, the university may believe the expense worthwhile, but the cost is real.

# Fund Raising

Fund raising is one of the research university's most important activities. Unlike almost every other program, the fund-raising office exists to deliver a large surplus to the university. Its goal is to keep its costs low and its earnings high because everything it earns through gifts, endowments, grants, and bequests returns to the university to support some activity.

Fund-raising organizations in private universities simply represent another administrative unit of the institution whose mission is to raise money. In public universities, however, with many restrictions on sources and uses of funds, the fund-raising unit often appears as a separate, not-for-profit foundation that exists to support the university but is not part of the bureaucratic or public activities of the institution. These foundations and fund-raising units do four things: they solicit and receive gifts, they supervise the investment of the endowment to ensure an adequate return, they monitor expenditures to be sure that the university follows the donors' wishes, and they report to the donors on the successful use of the gifts.

Fund raising is an absolutely critical dimension of every college and university, public or private, with increasingly sophisticated techniques and systems. Private colleges and universities have been much more engaged with fund raising over generations and have well-developed programs. In the last generation, most major public universities have developed capabilities rivaling all but the most seasoned private universities.

Some observers imagine that public universities could create sufficient private endowment and annual giving to replace state funding. While private philanthropy has helped many public universities with large endowments cope with state budget reductions, a complete conversion to private funding is usually not a realistic alternative. A relatively small part of the university's budget might come from the state, perhaps $300 million per year out of a total budget of perhaps $2 billion, or about 15 percent. To replace that $300 million, the development office would need to increase its endowment by an additional $6 billion (providing a payout of $300 million per year at 5 percent).

This target for additional fund raising is usually beyond the reach of public universities whose current budget already consumes the proceeds from its existing endowment to support the purposes of the various gifts. While endowment earnings and annual giving provide a significant enhancement to public university operations, they rarely can replace lost state funding or increase as fast as state dollars decline.

*How do I know what to ask for?* says the new president to his development officer as they prepare to visit a potential major new donor prospect, an alum who has been out of touch with the institution for many years. *How will I know what he's interested in?* The development officer says, *Ah, well, that's an art. You have to watch his eyes.* The president looks puzzled. *How does that work?* The development officer says, *Potential major donors are very smart; that's why they have money. They know you are there to ask. They usually want you to show that you care about them and their interests and that you have something they might like.* The president says, *Sure, but I won't know because we've not been in touch before.* The development officer responds, *But we do know he has an interest in the university, or we wouldn't have an appointment. Start talking about his time at the university, about the programs that have developed since then, about the opportunities in various areas, about the success of students and sports, and about the growth of campus facilities. In general, provide a short, conversational tour of the current university, its great future, and its significant past tied to his era.* The president says, *OK, I can do that, but how does that help me know what he cares about?* The development officer says, *You watch his eyes; when his eyes flicker, that's his interest.* The president asks, *And then what do I do?* The development officer says, *You keep right on talking, but in a bit circle back to that topic and develop it. Gradually you will find his interest grow as he begins to ask specific questions, and the focus of a relationship will appear.* The president says, *So the key is to watch their eyes and then ask for money? No,* says the development officer. *Watch their eyes and develop the relationship, but never ask for money until after the third to fifth visit.* The president says, *This is hard work. Yes,* says the development officer. *And remember, the conversation is always about the prospective donor and the university, not about you.*

## Intellectual Property

Research creates a stream of intellectual property from discoveries, inventions, and other intellectual products, some of which may have market value. The university has an obligation to put these results into the marketplace, where they can enhance commerce and the nation's competitiveness and recover whatever value is possible.

The most common forms of intellectual property involve patents, licenses, and in some cases royalties. The university patents discoveries with a commercial potential and then licenses them to companies with the capacity to further develop the discovery and turn it into a product. When the product succeeds, the resulting license income or royalty payment returns to the university inventors and the institution. The university portion is then reinvested in further research development.

Patent, license, and royalty income can create a significant source of marginal investment capital for most research universities, but the process of identifying commercially viable research is much more complicated and much less reliable than many people anticipate. Most scientific discoveries are not immediately, if ever, commercially viable. Many patents and licenses that belong to a university result in no income at all.

The occasional large commercial payout from a successful drug or a medical invention can lead observers to imagine that this activity could serve as core financial support for the institution. In reality, the commercialization of intellectual property is not reliable enough to base major university activities on the anticipated revenue stream. A significant research product such as specially developed seed for commercial crops can result in a substantial and continuing revenue stream, but even here, the varieties need to be constantly improved and updated to maintain their commercial viability.

The larger and more extensive a university's research activities, the more opportunities exist for successful commercialization. Much research is basic, dealing with fundamental properties of life or characteristics of the material world. While some of these may eventually become the basis for highly profitable products, the time and investment required to bring a discovery to market are substantial. The more research the university produces, the more opportunity it will have to find a commercial product within its results, but even then, the predictability of commercial success entails a high degree of risk.

## Libraries

The library is an iconic institution for most universities, traditionally standing at the center of the university's mission symbolizing the institutional commitment to the acquisition, transmission, sharing, and preservation of knowledge. Over the years, university libraries, and especially research university libraries, developed sophisticated systems for acquiring the materials faculty required for their research and assigned to students in support of their instructional mission. Libraries accumulated large collections of every kind of knowledge artifact, from audio recordings and computer files to rare books and manuscripts. Their systems grew ever more complex and computerized, with extensive linkages to national and worldwide resources of interest to faculty and students.

In recent years, the rapid acceleration of electronic services in support of library functions has challenged traditional assumptions about the role and purpose of the institutionally based library. Previously, a university library relied on the size, extent, and depth of the physical collection of books, serials, and other materials as tokens of the strength of the university's support for the academic enterprise. Universities also developed sharing arrangements through inter-library loans, for example, to reach required resources physically unavailable in the institutional repository.

Today, however, the proliferation of electronic resources has affected the publication of journals, some of which are available both online and in print and some of which are published online only. Aggregating services provide online access to large numbers of serial publications, and various e-book projects have been developed to transfer the physical materials of a library collection into electronic form theoretically accessible to everyone, everywhere. The electronic evangelists imagine a not very distant future where all materials of any interest to students, teachers, or researchers will reside in electronic formats, instantly accessible to users anywhere in the world. Although the technology to achieve this universal accessibility appears within reach, the infrastructure, organization, administration, and financing of such a universal virtual library have yet to fully appear.

In some fields, such as math, engineering, science, and medicine, the virtualization of published scholarship appears well along, although the financial arrangements and structure of authority and management are not yet stable. In fields less dependent on the journal article and more on the book, the digitization of monographs and other printed material is still very much under development.

For the library, the challenges are both organizational and financial. As the materials requested by library users become increasingly electronic, the library staff must acquire additional skills. Some specialists become obsolete and have been or will be replaced by professionals with different preparation. Traditional work patterns of interaction between librarians and users change dramatically with the shift of materials to remote electronic collections, and the physical space of libraries must go through a major reorientation. The primacy of printed reference and other materials, the importance of on-site physical presence for books and serials, and the role of facilitators such as reference librarians changes dramatically as the electronic revolution continues its inexorable progress.

All this carries with it a financial challenge, since electronic resources often cost more money and require more complex infrastructure. The transition, far from complete, requires the continued maintenance and development of current physical collections in addition to investment in new and often expensive electronic services. Librarians have made substantial advances in this conversion process from physical to electronic forms, but the transition is barely begun. Research university libraries have very large physical collections (a median collection is around four million volumes), and the challenges of converting these collections to electronic forms are substantial. At the same time, the users of the library, previously more closely focused on the common requirements for excellent service, appear to separate themselves into different sectors with substantially different priorities. The science, technology, and medical users see little need for much of the physical infrastructure, since their interest is in the rapid availability of new material through electronic access. Their interest in preservation and the custodial imperative of the library is minimal, since for them, what is old is mostly of limited interest. The humanists, many social scientists, and others who rely on books or on journals not yet fully in electronic form remain committed to the library's traditional functions of acquiring, maintaining, and preserving physical journals and books. For many of these users, the availability of actual books and other physical materials is a requirement, and they have a strong commitment to the preservation of materials of any age.

The students, of course, seek information relevant to their immediate coursework, whether for research papers or for the reading assignments associated with instruction. They see the library as a service center, a location for group work, and a place to plug into the electronic world and access the materials they need. They want electronic texts and other materials, especially if they can be provided at lower cost. They use online reference resources and find the traditional in-person library reference service of much less importance.

All of these changes challenge universities to find the funds, identify the right solutions among many alternatives, modify their collection practices, and continue to serve their faculty and students in an uncertain environment. As a reference point, there are about 115 research libraries that participate in the Association of Research Libraries. The median total library expenditure of just over $12 million lies within a wide range from over $56 million to around $4 million. Electronic expenditures of all kinds today consume perhaps a third of the total for a median institution, but some universities can spend around half of their total library budgets on electronic resources while others devote as little as 10 percent or less.

Given the challenges of electronic access to scholarly materials and the commercial and financial issues that affect copyrights and ownership, most libraries will likely find the best strategy in focusing on the careful adaptation to standard practices as those appear. Much very expensive experimentation with novel approaches and systems will take place before a stable and standard library and information structure emerges, and the risks are most appropriately carried by institutions with significant financial strength.

## Other Activities

Universities also participate in research and development parks, collaborate with business and industry on a variety of projects including high-tech incubators, work with state agencies to provide a wide range of services, and engage in a continuing stream of nonacademic activities that draw on institutional strengths. As an example of these nonacademic activities, universities often serve as the location for movies or television shows that use their ambiance for context. In every case, the university seeks to ensure that these nonacademic activities serve institutional interests and recover any extra costs. In the best of all possible worlds, such work might produce a profit or some other tangible benefit to the institution.

Large universities can also find opportunities, and some risk, in the development of hotels and conference centers located on or near the campus. They can partner with developers to create retirement centers with programs sponsored by the university that create extended communities of university-related people affiliated with the institution. These initiatives, along with the occasional shopping center or clinical outpatient facilities, can generate revenue for the institution, but they also carry all the risks of the commercial marketplace.

*Chapter 14*

# Regulation and Governance

C ompetition and choices continue to define the American university in the twenty-first century. Universities compete for every resource of significance from quality students to superior faculty, from state tax dollars to federal grants and contracts, and from corporate support to private funds and endowment. Universities make choices about the use of these funds to enhance the institution's ability to improve and compete more effectively. Productivity and quality provide the twin engines of university competition.

- Productivity matters because it multiplies the value of every dollar spent and because it creates value for the university's customers and supporters.
- Quality matters because investors in university activities seek a quality as well as a low-cost product. Even though much rhetoric focuses on inexpensive education, the consumer, the best students, the faculty, the state, the granting agencies, and the donors all seek association with quality.

## Regulation

The competition among universities is fierce, and to restrain that competition as much as possible, the state and the guilds create a wide range of regulatory agencies. Public universities cope with much more regulation than private institutions, but all universities have some variety of regulatory oversight.

All universities suffer from accreditation. Accreditation, originally invented to identify fraudulent institutions and programs, has become the defender of education fads and the regulator of guild privileges.

At the university level, regional associations generally review institutions on a ten-year cycle with five-year updates in accord with a host of criteria of often questionable utility. Frequently these associations propagate the education orthodoxy of the moment and encourage member universities to embrace the current principles as the price of a favorable accreditation report. Institutions conform, for to do otherwise is to risk a negative report that will bring major difficulties from the federal and state authorities that require accreditation.

Other associations focused on particular faculty guilds use accreditation to distort university funding priorities by demanding more equipment and space, more extensive support services, and lower student-to-faculty ratios than may actually be necessary for a quality product. Again, because accreditation is often required for governmental recognition, institutions distort their allocation structures to respond to the association's blackmail on behalf of its membership guilds.

While universities often resist the arbitrary standards of accreditation, they also use the accreditation process to leverage added resources from reluctant legislators or other program supporters. This restrains the push of many legislatures to reduce the cost of instruction because the university makes it clear that accreditation will be lost if funding falls too low. The regulatory dance between universities, accreditation associations, funding agencies, legislatures, and federal agencies constitutes one of the more expensive and labor-intensive bureaucratic activities of the institution.

States almost always have complex regulatory systems for public universities and some oversight over private institutions. No matter how the state institutions are organized, the state will limit opportunities, divide academic missions, and otherwise attempt to regulate competition and reduce duplication. All this they do in pursuit of economy and access, but instead they often achieve programmatic monopolies, extra-cost bureaucratic manipulation, and politicized systems.

No public university lives in a free-market economy, but the range of market responsiveness varies. In some systems, the institution controls tuition and the legislature controls appropriations; in others, the legislature or the executive branch and governor control all aspects of funding and expenditure. Most quality and productivity advances come when the university can be held accountable and is then left to compete, but many state institutions prefer the safety, political manipulation, and inefficiency of regulated environments to the competition and risk of an open market economy.

The federal government also regulates many aspects of university operations, from laws affecting affirmative action and financial aid to rules about athletics and research funding. The national research agenda exercises a powerful influence over the operation of university research environments, and federal rules determine much about the funding and management of university-based research.

Universities maintain substantial lobbying enterprises at federal and state levels to influence this regulatory environment. In addition, from time to time, various agencies of the federal government from the executive branch through the Congress generate studies, commissions, hearings, and other activities designed to promote a particular educational or political agenda.

## Governance

All universities have governance. Governance appears in many forms, some useful, some benign, and some destructive. The topic of governance means many things to different constituencies.

- To the faculty, governance means faculty involvement in and control over many aspects of university life, from academic issues of curriculum and hiring, including promotion and tenure, to budgetary allocations.
- To the students, it normally means the mechanisms that regulate student life, the power and authority of the student government, and the ability of students to influence institutional policies and practices. It includes student influence over the rules governing many extracurricular activities and in many institutions the operation of the Greek system of fraternities and sororities.
- In private universities, governance refers almost always to boards of trustees who have final authority for the university and responsibility for its operations, although private universities also have faculty and student governance organizations.
- In public universities, governance also means boards of regents, trustees, or supervisors, governors, education commissioners, higher education commissions, and legislatures. All assert some form of governance control over the institution.
- To administrative staff, governance may mean the organization of the university's bureaucracy that establishes reporting relationships and lines of authority.

All of these participants assert a governance role and responsibility within the context of university operations. Sorting out this complex structure of authority and responsibility is never easy, and while some commonalities exist in all university governance arrangements, local variations tend to be many and significant.

## Governing Boards

All universities have governing boards, and some have more than one. A governing board (whether of regents or trustees or supervisors—the nomenclature is mostly without significance) generally serves as the ultimate authority for the university, the location from which all power and authority flows and the place to which all accountability returns. While its primary role may be fiduciary, ensuring the financial stability of the institution, most governing boards have wide power and extensive authority over all aspects of the institutional operation, although they usually delegate much of this authority to administrative and academic officers.

In the case of private universities, this description matches reality rather well. Private university boards, whose members may number sixty or more, serve to hire presidents, ensure the fiscal solvency of the university, and approve major policies. They often approve appointments of senior administrative officers on the recommendation of the president, they frequently approve tenure appointments on the recommendation of the faculty and the president, they almost always award degrees on the recommendation of the faculty and president, and in every case they expect to participate continuously and energetically in the fund-raising activities of the institution.

Private university boards generally have a tight focus on the specific issues of their university and recognize that their job is to assure the fiscal viability of the institution and promote the university's success. They are single-minded in these pursuits, and while they may make mistakes or fail to understand some issues, their interest in the university tends to be undivided.

Private boards are, for the most part, self-perpetuating, and they select and appoint their members, although in some instances there are student, faculty, and alumni representatives as members. In other instances, where a state provides significant financial support to a private institution, the governor may appoint a board member. Some boards have terms for their members, while others have indefinite appointments. Many qualities earn membership on these private university boards, but significant contributions to the university's welfare, often in the form of substantial donations, provide the most important qualification, followed by distinguished public service.

The board members often have a major financial investment in the success of the institution through their own large gifts to endowment or through family bequests. Private university boards tend to meet infrequently, perhaps quarterly, and do the majority of their work though their committee structure. In many cases, the president of the university serves as an ex-officio board member. Almost all university boards organize themselves into committees and subcommittees to do the work of the institution, and often the major direction of the board comes from its chair and its executive and finance committees.

Public university boards are much different. These boards in almost all cases are politically created, although the mechanisms for their creation vary. In some states, the legislature or the governor appoints the members; in a few the board members stand for public election. Many states give the authority of appointment to the governor and confirmation of that appointment to the legislature. In others, the university's board has elected alumni members in addition to politically appointed members. Many boards have student members, who are normally appointed by the governor but sometimes elected by the students.

The variations on these themes are many. In some states with complex university systems, a single board supervises all universities. In these cases, the board is really external to the university and has its own bureaucratic support structure with an executive officer called either "chancellor" or "president" depending on tradition (the other name usually applies to the institutional head).

Some systems have an overarching board at the state level and then individual university boards. Or a state may have several multiple university systems as well as a coordinating board. In other cases, each university in a system has a board of advisors or trustees, but authority resides primarily in a higher-level state board. In these cases, the university board may be without significant authority, serve primarily as a fund-raising and lobbying entity, and participate in the recruitment and selection of campus presidents or chancellors.

In the public sector, in most cases, the members of a university's governing board do not have a single focus on the university's best interests but instead serve multiple masters, from governor to legislators and other special constituencies. In multiuniversity boards, the members often have geographic loyalties and serve not only to seek the benefit of the system but also to protect and advance the specific political interests of their geographic region and the institutions within it.

Good public boards also serve to protect the university against legislative and executive-branch interference. Boards that respond too readily to the whims of elected officials or special interests of one kind or another do their institutions a great and damaging disservice. In theory independent and with extensive responsibilities, these public board members can serve the institutions well. However, because public universities have widely differing standings within the political and bureaucratic space of their respective states, and because they speak primarily to these local constituencies, generalizations about public university governance are difficult to make accurately.

In addition, because of their highly politicized nature, state university boards differ dramatically in their performance and effectiveness depending on the circumstances and personalities of the political moment. What works well in one political era may prove singularly ineffective in another. Given the appointment process of public university board members, it is not surprising to find them often more responsive to the interests of their external constituencies (governors, legislators, and various special interests) than to the academic success of the institutions they supervise. Indeed, it is fair to say that one of the most important differences between the public board and the private board is that the public board exists to regulate the university within some concept of the public interest while the private board exists to maximize the university's performance and support its work.

Public university boards generally have many of the same powers as the private board but have less complete control of the institutions, and the board itself must respond to multiple laws, rules, regulations, and other constraints placed on it by the political history and structure of the state. In some states, universities are constitutional, and their existence derives from state constitutional provisions. Those universities and their boards tend to have somewhat more autonomy from the intervention of state legislatures and governors than universities that exist by virtue of a state law, but the independence is often more a function of political climate than formal authority.

When the university is a creature of the legislature, changes in its status, functions, autonomy, and authority require only the action of the legislature and the governor, as is the case with any state law. When the university is a constitutional entity, however, the legislature can still have great influence, but it cannot change the basic powers and authority of the institution without invoking the process of constitutional change, an often difficult and unpredictable activity. In these cases, the legislature often uses the power of the purse through the appropriation process to achieve its goals.

Public universities exist to serve the public interest as defined by their boards, legislatures, and governors. Private universities, while they too serve the public interest, define the public interest on their own terms. Most private universities can be more focused, effective, and consistent over time because they are not as easily subject to temporary, local political enthusiasms as are the public institutions.

The chair of the board of trustees calls the president. *What's this I read in the paper about the university planning to close programs as state funding declines?* The president answers, *Well, you remember our discussion of the budget at the last board meeting. We've lost 25 percent of state funding over the last three years, and we must now readjust the university's budget to meet our income. Yes,* says the chair, *but the governor's staff called and wants to be sure that we do nothing that can be blamed on the governor. Mr. Chairman,* the president responds, *we may not blame the governor, but the students and faculty whose programs must be reduced may have a different approach. Well, Mr. President, you need to manage the reductions so there is no public fallout. But Mr. Chairman,* says the president, *that will prevent us from making the changes that are essential for the effective operation of the university. Mr. President,* says the chairman, *you have your instructions.*

## Faculty Governance

Governance for faculty defines their engagement in the decision process of the institution. In general, although variations are many and significant, faculty have primary authority over the curriculum, the general academic standards of the institution, the definition of degrees, and the approval of candidates for degrees. Faculty also have the most influence over the hiring, promotion, and tenure of faculty. These all represent primarily guild functions, and most universities recognize the faculty's authority, although in many institutions the law and other administrative rules inhibit the faculty's freedom of action in some of these areas.

The mechanisms of faculty governance are guild-like and consist primarily of committees, councils, and senates (representative or participatory in nature). These collections of faculty, defined primarily by guild criteria, exist at all levels, from the departmental faculty meeting to the university-wide faculty council or senate. The rights and responsibilities of the faculty normally exist in written form in a faculty constitution or handbook that describes the faculty's rights, how they are to exercise those rights, and who has the ability to overrule the faculty. In most universities, the president or chancellor (and of course the governing board) have the right to overrule the faculty on almost all matters, but they only do so with good reason and relatively infrequently when dealing with core guild matters.

Faculty also want to be involved in fiscal and budgetary matters. In this, university practice varies. Most universities permit the faculty to have an opinion, to have a committee that takes cognizance of the university's financial issues, and perhaps to offer opinions and counsel, but almost no university gives the faculty the right to manage the money. This is because the faculty are not responsible for the money. Authority and responsibility belong together, and so the trustees of both public and private institutions insist on clear lines of fiscal authority and responsibility, for if these boards have one obligation it is for the fiscal solvency of the institution.

The rise of the labor union movement has also had a significant impact on issues of faculty governance. Labor unions of the variety of AFT, UAW, NEA, or AAUP take the industrial trade union movement as their model and proletarianize the faculty's economic issues. These are mostly concerns about workload, salary, and benefits, although other issues sometimes come into play. In many institutions, the unions carefully avoid engaging in academic guild matters, restricting themselves to major workplace and compensation issues.

One consequence of the union movement has been a decline in the power of faculty governance in other areas. Because money matters, the administration and the union resolve money matters outside of the normal, guild-driven traditional faculty governance system. On other issues of guild importance, faculty governance has less significance because the participants are not also participants in conversations about money.

Unions resolve many difficult issues for administrators. With a union, grievance issues no longer fall into a settlement mode dominated by guild-like faculty committees but instead fall into a labor union mode dominated by bureaucratic rules of procedure, essentially a civil service type of conflict resolution. This offers protections to the faculty in many cases, but it also makes it easy for administrators to ignore faculty academic concerns that may be part of grievances because the bureaucratic rules and union contract provide a ritualized path for resolution.

The principal leadership of the faculty, however, does not only come from the councils and governance organizations. Deans and department chairs carry the faculty voice in the conversation about university policy and procedures. They are the intermediaries between the corporate nature of the university and the guild spirit of the faculty. While they speak for and on behalf of the guilds, they serve at the pleasure of the corporation. Consequently, they represent the transfer point between the guild's ancient academic traditions and the corporate university shell's competitive, commercial, labor union, and market-driven imperatives.

Although often seen as relatively ineffective, the faculty voice in university affairs can, in times of crisis or challenges to the integrity of the institution, become loud and powerful. Usually, these moments are issue related, and the faculty power generated by a crisis dissipates rather quickly.

## Student Government

Students in all universities have their own agenda. They want low tuition, an active campus life, and authority over or at least a significant voice in all aspects of university management that affect students. They think they should participate in guild issues such as promotion and tenure, they believe they should help allocate the budget, they expect to help drive the curriculum, and in most cases they know that student life with its complex functions and large budget is both their responsibility and their base of power.

Students operate through many organizations, the principal one being student government. In most large public universities, student government is controlled by a relatively small fraction of politically active students and primarily by already organized students through fraternity and sorority structures, where those exist, and by other affinity groups capable of mobilizing the relatively few students required to win student government elections, which are generally characterized by low turnout.

In addition, special focus groups of students organize and lobby. These include women's groups, gay and lesbian associations, environmental activists, black student unions, Hispanic student associations, Asian student associations, Libertarian student groups, Democratic or Republican student clubs, or recreation-oriented student groups for rock climbing, hiking, and other similar activities. Some of these are constituency groups of long standing, institutionalized by the university in such entities as black student unions, Hispanic student associations, women's centers, or intramural sports associations.

Others arise as ad hoc organizations in support of a particular cause such as environmental or labor issues. Whatever their origin, these subunits of the student population lobby both the established student government for more money and involvement and the university for more influence over policies related to their particular concerns.

Students obviously have a different frame of reference from other university actors. Their time at the institution is relatively short compared to a faculty career or the terms of many significant university administrators. They tend to be impatient, and their focus will often be concentrated on hot-button issues of particular relevance to the moment.

Other university actors, whether unions or faculty groups or outside interests seeking to influence university behavior, will on occasion use students to further a particular agenda, recognizing that students occupy a special place in the university's concerns. Students often bring national and international issues of significance inside the university, where they know they can control a forum and make significant and highly visible statements.

Over the years, and especially since the late 1960s and early 1970s, universities have developed some experience and skill at differentiating between student issues associated with teaching and research and those responding to external campaigns. However, because universities are always engaged in the larger issues of the society that supports them, what may appear to be an external issue will often develop into a campaign with an impact on the content and operation of the university itself.

## Governance Operation

Within this structure, the governance of the institution takes place in accord with written policies and procedures as well as traditions. Public universities tend to have many bureaucratic structures with many written rules and regulations, which are often designed to protect the institution against the intervention of outside political influences. The public university uses the bureaucratic process of rule creation and enforcement to buffer the many political microconstituencies that seek advantage, opportunity, or platform within the institution.

Because the public university's authority is weak and derived in most cases from a potentially volatile political process, the rule-making system creates safe havens for decisions that will make some constituency unhappy. Since large public universities have many constituencies, almost every decision has the potential to generate a political controversy. The rules and procedures through which the university implements decisions buffer these controversies and usually, but not always, permit the institution to do what needs to be done.

*Policy formation* at major universities is both complicated and varied. Some universities have well-ordered structures for making policy that involve councils, meetings, and other representation articulated through formal procedures. Most universities, however, have traditions and expected behaviors for making policy decisions.

Part of the policy process involves deciding in whose domain the content of the policy falls. If it is fiscal, it belongs primarily in the administrative shell's domain; if it involves curriculum and academic standards, it falls primarily in the faculty guild's domain. If it affects students, the student government or student interest groups will be involved. But most policies actually involve all three.

If the university changes its academic standards in some way, the change is likely to have a fiscal impact (more or fewer students, more or fewer faculty). If the university changes its fiscal policies in some way, that change is likely to have an academic impact (if we spend more on deferred maintenance we may spend less on the library; by spending more on parking we may spend less on laboratory equipment). Further, students take a keen interest in these issues, and often student interests and faculty interests do not coincide (students want low tuition, but the university wants to raise tuition to raise faculty salaries; students want more recreation space, but faculty want more laboratory space). As a result, the process of university governance involves a wide range of complex negotiations, meetings, and consultations, all designed to buffer the conflicting interests.

In some states, the role of the *public media* looms large in the university's decision process as various factions manipulate the media's enthusiasm for controversy to influence particular internal outcomes. Through the agency of aggressive public records and public meeting laws, the media become participants in the decision process of the public university under the guise of informing the public. In these contexts, the press and other media outlets serve primarily to exaggerate conflict, minimize consensus, encourage cynicism, and stifle open discussion.

The rise of social media created a new public forum for controversy and discussion. On occasion, a change in university policies, organization, or purpose will release an almost instantaneous firestorm of Twitter, Facebook, and other Internet-enabled forms of controversy. Most familiar to those who follow the ups and downs, rumors and gossip related to college sports, this same high-intensity and often stylistically extreme electronic media response can on occasion upset the orderly process of institutional governance. The best approach is always careful preparation in anticipation that nothing proposed will pass unnoticed.

The public nature of complex discussions in this environment encourages university people to conduct their business off book, out of the formal processes, and off the public record. This makes the process less visible, and it makes the visible process a less accurate reflection of the issues. It often moves the discussion from the structured forums of the academy into a brokered discussion through the media or into backroom negotiations among insiders.

Aggressive press exposure eliminates the thoughtful voices of faculty, administrators, or trustees who may have a doubt from the conversation, and it substitutes for them the manipulative voices of those who take extreme positions based on dogmatic certainty or those who seek visibility in the media for other purposes. It also eliminates from the conversation those individuals who do not choose to do their thinking in public.

The more aggressive and effective the public record and open meeting laws, the less effective the collegial activities of the guild will be. Different observers will have a different evaluation of the cost-benefit ratio associated with opening all the university's activities to the press. Private universities, of course, do not suffer as much from this, and many states have reasonable limits on what is open and what is confidential.

University governance structures show a decided bias toward inaction. Complexity and bureaucracy, especially in the public sector, tend to absorb initiatives for change and dissipate them across a wide estuary of bureaucratic swamps and regulatory tributaries so that the flow of change slows to a virtual stop. The process, however, is constructed so that as the flow of change is captured, it gives up its energy in an often dramatic, or at least showy, display of verbal pyrotechnics. Committee reports, statements of intent, high-sounding charges to committees, thoughtful consultations, multiple reports and data displays, press publicity—all these are the foam of change dissipating in the estuary of inertia.

In the public sector, governance does not require change because survival floats on an entitlement tide of undergraduate students. Unless the undergraduates go somewhere else, a public university of any significant size is protected against much significant change, absent a dramatic state fiscal crisis.

Private universities also resist change, for they too live through their guilds. But in the private sector, for most universities, the entitlement of endowment is often not enough to ensure the scale of a major university, and so the faculty, students, and administration, while they may not always agree, recognize the realities of the marketplace within which they compete. They tend to be more focused on the economic structure of the academic world. No less self-absorbed than their public university counterparts, they nonetheless recognize that the economic success of the university rests on their shoulders and not primarily on the largess of the taxpaying public.

Part of the difference between public and private university behavior reflects the rate of change. In the public sector, universities resist change until some event forces a relatively significant readjustment (a downturn in the economy, a budget cut, a legislative outburst). In the private sector, where each year is a challenge to earn the revenue that will ensure guild prosperity, change comes incrementally, as needed and as the demand for academic goods and services dictates. Consequently, private universities often appear changeless precisely because they must be constantly changing in pursuit of comparative advantage within their marketplaces.

Nonetheless, even private universities at times become lost in their own worlds and lose sight of the realities that surround them. They can defer maintenance and keep faculty salaries high until a crisis demands a budget readjustment to fix the decaying and now dangerous buildings. They can borrow money to build elegant facilities in anticipation of donation dollars or enrollment growth that never arrive, waking up one day to the need for dramatic readjustments to meet unavoidable fiscal consequences.

Private universities, because they live on their own revenue and because they depend on their administration and their trustees to keep them sound, live in a riskier world than public universities, surrounded as they are by multiple watchers and accountants and critics. Private universities, for the most part exempt from public records legislation, can often keep their institutional crises from the public media, although from time to time a crisis reaches such magnitude that it surfaces into public view. Usually, but with notable exceptions, the public notice of such a crisis involves smaller private colleges with fewer resources to buffer failures or misjudgments. Governance, then, is a complex and fascinating topic for those interested in the micropolitics of small societies.

*Chapter 15*

# Disruptive Change

--------------------------------------------------------

U niversities and their many constituencies have a tradition and commitment to worry. In cycles of five to ten years, changes in the world, the expansion or contraction of U.S. and world economies, the dynamics of war and peace, the emergence of challenging cultural trends, and the development of new technologies all trigger intense self-examination and concern.

The higher education community anticipates great changes, worries about uncontrolled or unanticipated shifts in higher education traditions, seeks better predictions of future market conditions, struggles to adapt to new technology or shifting demographics, and fears major readjustments in the financial base of their institutions. To some extent, these concerns are a normal part of academic life and have been for generations. Although one might imagine that the long trajectory of the university as a key component of Western life would give comfort to those who worry, many people nonetheless envision the end of the university "as we know it."

In almost all cases, the causes for worry are genuine and reflect real changes in the environment within which universities have prospered. The shifting economic structure of global commerce and its impact on the U.S. economy is a real transformation. The pervasive injection of high technology into the everyday operations of our society and its workplace, including the university, has forced and will continue to force changes in operations and values. Demographic shifts that change the characteristics and aspirations of the college-attending population and economic restructuring that transfers jobs of varying skill levels into and out of the United States have an impact on higher education.

These changes, and many others, challenge the university. They have motivated and they will continue to motivate considerable evolution of markets and operations for many institutions of higher education. Yet the assumption that this moment in world history is more revolutionary and more disruptive of university life than previous crises experienced by the United States is likely exaggerated. We all may believe that we live in unusually challenging times and that our crises are special and more critical than those that have come before. We should take comfort in looking backward to see that the dramatic events of a generation or so ago in the late 1960s and early 1970s, which many participants at the time believed presaged the end of the university as they knew it, nonetheless left universities much as they were before.

Universities are exceptionally stable enterprises and continuously adaptable. They modify and rearrange themselves to meet the challenges posed in each succeeding generation, never changing quickly enough to satisfy their critics or, indeed, more quickly than is required by the circumstances around them. Over time, universities acquire new attributes, goals, and constituencies while discarding others. These changes almost never occur all at once in a cataclysmic disruption but rather gradually, idiosyncratically, and unpredictably over time. Such has been the history of these remarkable institutions, and it is likely to continue for quite some time in the same fashion.

This relatively slow adjustment to the world and the immediate society around universities comes from the actions of individuals, institutions, and university constituencies focusing on different elements of the institutional environment at varying times. We can identify some of the change agents and, by looking at various current university responses, perhaps gain some perspective on future transformations.

## Technology

The impact of technology on all businesses worldwide has been pervasive, substantial, and in many cases revolutionary. The Internet, computerized manufacturing, robotics, large-scale business management, sophisticated financial instruments, cell phones, the endless variety of computing devices, and many more manifestations of the expansion of technology have modified the scale and organizational complexity of many social, political, and commercial activities. These transformations have affected the nature of commerce, globalizing much of what used to be local and transforming the value of labor. The divergence of skill levels between functions that require minimal levels and those that require advanced levels has contributed to the growing disparity in income distribution around the world.

The most affected enterprises are those that benefit from scale and speed of transaction; the least affected are service industries that provide value through more or less individualized personal interactions. This helps explain the widely varying response of higher education to the transformations that have had such a profound effect elsewhere in the world economy.

Universities, in their traditional and elite form, represent a special category of individualized transaction that links teachers and students in small numbers to achieve a high-touch interaction perceived to be of great value. This format does not scale well, and as universities grow in size and scope they often lose the personalized transaction value that many of their customers prize. For this reason, traditional universities rarely grow much beyond an enrollment of forty to fifty thousand students before splitting into smaller subunits that are separately operated and administered.

Computers and technology innovation are common parts of all universities and colleges today, but so far, they have mostly enhanced, modified, improved, and facilitated the personalized interaction rather than supplanting it in any systematic fashion. Some forms of computer-assisted instruction relieve faculty and students of routine work related to such things as beginning writing, some math instruction, and similar beginning-level, routine teaching. However, the success of large-scale, computer-driven postsecondary enterprises has been most evident in nonstandard, nonelite educational settings.

Distance education (a misnomer since distance is not required for computer-mediated instruction) provides access to higher education content for many students unable or uninterested in the high-touch traditional structure. It reaches students whose work schedules do not permit regular attendance at real-time classes, whose interaction with higher education is episodic and dependent on circumstances that change from semester to semester, and whose place-bound location prohibits involvement in campus-based classes. These individuals and many others with similar requirements take advantage of the computer-mediated instruction that has grown increasingly sophisticated over the last decade.

While traditional colleges and universities participate in these ventures, they tend to do so on the margin to capture new markets, serve hard-to-reach students, connect with elite, high-revenue-producing constituencies in business or industry, or augment campus-based instructional programs. Currently, this environment is much in flux.

As the technology and delivery systems develop and mature, more potential student markets appear possible. However, the financial structure of distance education does not always produce significant profits or even recover the initial investment or operating costs. Quality is expensive here as well as everywhere else in higher education, and it takes a considerable investment to produce high-quality materials and support. Over the years, some institutions have developed quite successful and profitable distance education operations, and we can expect to see more of these emerge as the technology becomes standardized and the techniques to ensure quality and effectiveness become better developed.

These systems may well provide just as good higher education at a lower cost and greater convenience to large numbers of students. Some see this as a major threat to higher education in its traditional campus-based mode, but the threat depends on the sector of higher education involved. The impact of computer-mediated, noncampus higher education is likely to be much greater on the less prestigious institutions than on the elite, highly selective colleges and universities. Those below the top level of selectivity provide functional, effective education that serves their students well. The expensive, high-touch style of traditional colleges and universities may well be less important for the students of these institutions, especially as the cost of higher education continues to rise and the attractiveness of less expensive e-learning options increases.

Middle-level colleges and universities are likely to find themselves involved in both on-campus and distance or e-learning educational modalities, creating a balance that allows them to maintain the context of the traditional model (which has significant brand enhancing value) while at the same time reaching markets they need for survival and prosperity through increasingly sophisticated computer-mediated instruction. The emergence of specialized service agencies that establish and operate distance education platforms to carry any university's instructional program and brand lowers the entry barrier to high-quality Internet-enabled education. For-profit entrepreneurs also have found this modality effective, in large part because the not-for-profit institutions do not yet compete vigorously in the same space. Once they do, it is not clear whether the for-profits will be able to extract the premium from this market that will satisfy their investors.

Elite institutions also seek to engage new markets and experiment with innovative techniques. Some post elements of their instructional programs online for free, offering materials and various forms of instruction at no or minimal cost. Some experiments include course-like processes with forms of automated grading and completion certificates but as yet no degrees. Whether the prestigious institutions will find this an eventually profitable online product (in much the same way prestigious newspapers began posting content online for free and then erected pay walls to capture the commercial value of their brand and products) remains to be seen.

Additional experiments take the traditional engagement of American universities in recruiting international students to a new level by creating name-brand branch facilities in overseas locations where significant profitability appears possible. These are high-risk ventures, but they promise great reward for successful initiatives.

Much of this activity is still quite preliminary and involves primarily high-prestige institutions with substantial economic resources. It also, however, demonstrates the concern at all levels of American higher education about developing the means of expanding scale and competing globally. As with all new ventures, many of these will fail, but some will succeed, leading others to imitate the process.

The technological revolution has not run its course or become institutionalized in a stable form, and we can expect continued experimentation, expansion, and failure. One of the lessons of past initiatives is that innovations of this kind are best tested by organizations and universities with the resources to lose money. Once a technological innovation has been tested and found stable and cost effective, less wealthy institutions can capture its value. The importance of being first to market is relatively low in higher education.

> *Chancellor,* says the enthusiastic trustee, *I'm worried that we're not keeping up.* The chancellor, recognizing the sound of an incoming rocket, asks, *In what way? Well,* says the trustee, *I've been reading about the impact of Big Data, the importance of Crowd Sourcing, the implementation of learning in the Cloud, Massive Open Online Communities, Large-Scale E-Learning platforms, and Digital Archives. I understand that universities are in a period of Dynamic, Disruptive change, and we do not want to be caught unprepared at this Tipping Point.* The chancellor, reeling from the sequence of buzzwords and trendy jargon, buys some time by saying, *These are surely important issues. What do you think we should do?* The trustee says, *We should create new initiatives with innovative programs to stay with the leaders.* The chancellor thinks, but does not say, *This is nuts. We are making progress doing what makes us better and more competitive within our mission and our resources. Following these trendy ideas, all of which are expensive and most of which will not work, will take money away from improving our competitive position.* Instead, reflecting the trustee's enthusiasm for buzz phrases, she says, *Mr. Trustee, these are very important themes, and we'll put together a task force to review the best way to take advantage of the perfect storm coming our way.* Reassured by the chancellor's recognition of the impending crisis he has identified, the trustee moves on to talk about the football season.

## Demographics

The economic restructuring of world commerce and industry has carried with it a significant change in American demographics. There are many demographic changes throughout the world as well, but our concern here is with the American university. We are not a nation with a rapidly growing college-aged population. High school graduates prepared for college are not a rapidly expanding group, and their number may decline in some areas of the country. At the same time, the proportion of the population that believes a college degree is an essential entry credential to a good middle-class life continues to increase.

Some of this is a rational response to the decline of well-paying middle-income jobs in industries where technology and offshore manufacturing have reduced the number of desirable positions. The economic downturn and slow recovery of 2008–2012 further eroded the job market for people without specialized skills.

These economic changes have increased the demand for various kinds of postsecondary education and have had the most impact on community colleges, for-profit colleges, nonelite private colleges, and middle-range state colleges. These institutions, always focused extensively on students for whom a college degree represented a job access credential, have found themselves overwhelmed in many cases by students seeking the training that would qualify them for a better job. Some of the potential students at this level came with substandard secondary preparation, increasing the remedial work required for success and often increasing the failure rate of those who attempted college-level work.

At prestigious, highly selective colleges and universities, these job forces reinforce the value of elite, high-touch education. The upper middle class and above seek entry into prestigious institutions ever more aggressively, recognizing that the divergence of income in the United States requires the next generation to be firmly in at least the upper-middle income level to sustain a reasonable middle-class lifestyle. This results in an intense competition for places in highly selective colleges and universities.

While the competition for places in elite colleges and universities responds to many of the same global changes in the labor market as the growth in enrollment at community and technical colleges and at state colleges and universities, the purpose of the education sought differs. Elite colleges and universities prepare students in the traditional, primarily liberal arts mode (enhanced by preprofessional training for business, medicine, and law), and their graduates often see themselves headed for postgraduate study leading to professional degrees and high-value professional careers. Job placement at graduation may be an expected outcome of an elite college education for those who do not choose to pursue advanced professional or academic training; it is usually not the primary goal of an elite undergraduate education.

The particular value of elite institutions lies in their high-touch, individualized instructional modes. Even in the large public elite institutions, personalized instruction at the upper levels and through honors and other specialized subgroupings within the university provide this value. Some elite institutions experiment with distance education and a number of other large-scale interaction enterprises (free courses on the Internet, for example), but they do so from a secure elite base. Basically, they trade on the high value of their brands to commercialize their reputations into alternative markets.

## International Competition

With the expansion of commerce, industry, technology, and science into a world commodity environment, the role of elite higher education and especially research-driven institutional development has grown ever greater. As region after region and country after country seeks the economic and commercial benefits of high-powered university research and development, the competition for quality faculty and the investment in research capacity has grown significantly.

Some of this is visible through the high-profile proliferation of ranking schemes designed to promote or distinguish internationally competitive research institutions within various countries. This competition draws much of its inspiration from the impact of the American model of research university development. While each country has its own traditions and mechanisms for identifying and promoting international research competence, the critical element is the general agreement about what constitutes quality and performance. Publications of scientific merit are the coin of the international marketplace for research, and that coin is denominated primarily in English, reflecting the dominance of United States and some European institutions in establishing the conditions and structure of the marketplace for high-quality scientific research.

Like the business, technological, and industrial baseline of international competition, research tends increasingly to divest itself of cultural context. Science is science wherever it occurs, just as computing power is computing power everywhere. Science results published in peer-reviewed journals are tested, applied, developed, and expanded in universities regardless of their national origins and context. The success of the international university depends on the success of its research products finding a worldwide audience.

Although we humanists may regret the deculturation of higher education institutions, the benefit for the United States is that the model pursued by most international competitors is primarily a U.S. model of research university operation. This means that top U.S. institutions have well-developed, advanced platforms for competition, but it also means that their international competitors are constantly seeking ways to improve on those models to compete more effectively.

Given the importance of science and technology (writ large to include highly scalable business enterprises and mechanisms for transport and merchandising) in driving the current version of world commerce and trade, we anticipate that the top

American research universities will continue to compete successfully in this marketplace. We also anticipate that some number of those just below the top level may find it difficult to sustain the investment essential for preeminent participation in the world marketplace.

## Financial Structure

In all these considerations, as has been clear throughout this little book, what matters is the money. Money determines what kind of education we deliver to whom and under what circumstances. Given the financial challenges of the public sector in the United States, it seems likely that the ability of states to continue to support major research universities at the level and in the number that currently exist will decline. Some of the current public participants at the top or just below the top level of research competition will likely slowly decline in competitiveness.

This does not mean that others will take their place. Instead, it is likely that the gap between the truly internationally competitive United States research universities and those that are merely good will widen significantly. There will be no dramatic transformation of the research university environment. The top producers will stay in place, but the second tier will gradually fall behind as they fail to generate the continuing investment required to sustain premier research performance.

Private elite research universities may well survive this transition better than many public elite institutions, in part because their financial structures are more diversified and in part because private universities are in general more efficient, more tightly focused, and more capable of rapid change than their public counterparts. The public institutions, constrained as they are by the political cultures of their states and the continuing obligations of large student populations, will in many cases struggle to compete.

The nonelite sectors of higher education will continue to diversify by type, instructional characteristics, technology, and market niche. The demand for occupation-specific education will increase in these sectors, the standards imposed for public accountability will become lower but more specific, and the competition for funding will continue to be intense.

Within this context, the most challenged institutions will be nonelite, private liberal arts institutions or small public colleges and universities with fewer than five thousand students. These institutions will find it very difficult to maintain sufficient student numbers to sustain effective operations and to command high enough prices to pay the costs associated with their limited scale.

## Disaggregation of Content and Context

Many of the challenges we see in the postsecondary marketplace come from a rapid disaggregation of content from the context of information, learning, and instruction. In the classical liberal arts college model, content and context exist bound tightly together, each supporting and enhancing the value of the other. Students live, socialize, eat, sleep, study, write, read, discuss, attend class, and learn within a carefully constructed environment that defines all these activities, intellectual, social, and experiential, as essential to the quality of the resulting college education.

Alongside this coherent vision of an educational experience, we have always operated continuing and distance education programs aimed at different demographically or geographically defined groups. These programs have delivered the content of our academic expertise absent the elaborate residential and experiential context of the core college or university life. With the growth of technology and the increasing demand for more postsecondary education, e-learning platforms have further refined and extended the reach of content-specific education that is tailored to deliver content when and where needed with the minimum of context. The more sophisticated the e-learning system, the less real-time context appeared necessary. Some institutions, recognizing the opportunities for increasing the leverage of existing faculty and other instructional talent, began delivering some portions of their content directly to residential students using e-learning platforms and techniques.

Students and other consumers of higher education services also found it possible to purchase elements of the context without any requirement to engage the content. Entertainment venues on campus for concerts of every variety from rock and country to opera and ballet became accessible to audiences with no affiliation with the content of the university. Elaborate sports venues and events drew multitudes of consumers in person or via television to enjoy a presumably student-driven event filled with college context but absent any academic content. Indeed, intercollegiate sports at all levels are perhaps the best examples of content-free collegiate context sold to unaffiliated or only partially affiliated audiences.

Other elements of this separation of content from context come from the rise and expansion of certificate-based programs, content activities focused explicitly on the acquisition of job-specific skills valuable in the marketplace. These programs, whether conducted online or on site, also exist with minimum context and maximum content. They are designed to deliver essential training and justify a certificate of competence within the shortest possible time. Aimed often at adult students for whom the social context of the residential university or college has much less value or at students for whom the baccalaureate degree is less desirable than a competency certificate, these programs have proliferated and established significant markets.

Many less-selective colleges and universities (both public and private) operate in a hybrid mode that sustains an on-campus collegiate context for some portion of their customers. These institutions will likely rely even more in the future on revenue from providing context-free content through e-learning and other modalities of education to audiences with widely varying requirements. Some of these customers will seek traditional college degrees, but more and more will identify those skills for which a certification of competence adds value to the individual's pursuit of enhanced career opportunities.

Highly selective institutions, where context is a major feature and a product of high value to many constituents, find themselves in something of a challenging position. They recognize the markets accessible to institutions that can unbundle the content from the context and sell information and training to large audiences, many perhaps overseas. They also understand that merchandising their high-touch brands by associating them with context-free training has the potential to tarnish the bright prestige of their core operations. Some experiment with carefully crafted programs that reach beyond the campus but position themselves as offering campus quality and results, even if at a remote distance. Others offer programs that build in as much computer-mediated context as possible through lecture capture, synchronous, video-enhanced discussion sections, and other quasi-live enhancements.

Some prestigious institutions offer their content without context but also without associating the institutional brand with the product, simply providing a window into the content without assuming responsibility for the quality of the participant's engagement. Others join collaborative enterprises that carry newly minted names and contribute their intellectual content but do not directly associate their brand with the new collaborative, context-free product.

These strategies, most still in experimental modes, seek to preserve the high cost and high value of the exclusive context provided by the residential, physical place while nonetheless capturing some of the new revenue and the aura of progressive innovation associated with the context-free online world.

Although it is not yet clear how these experiments will develop or what the stable restructured marketplace for postsecondary content and context will look like, we can be sure that the context-free, disaggregated educational providers will continue to grow, their markets will likely expand, and as they develop sophisticated methods of quality control, the value of their certification process will increase.

There is nothing more gratifying than predicting the future, for no future facts contradict the predictions. Some of these transformations may be highly disruptive to some parts of the higher education industry, but they may also reinforce others. All must cope with the changes identified above and many we have surely missed, but the adaptations of elite research institutions will be much different than those required of other colleges and universities.

## Chapter 16

# People

-----------------------------------------------------------

U niversities, like most of postsecondary education, are people enterprises. The strong structures of the American research university prototype, with its academic core and administrative shell, the critical requirements for money, the essential structure of budgets, and the careful management of guilds, serve one primary function: the acquisition, management, support, and retention of high-quality people.

While beautiful grounds with their timeless buildings, large libraries, complex scientific facilities, great sports stadiums, and elegant student recreation centers impress all who visit these charmed places, the less easily viewed, but by far most important, university assets are its people. Universities employ a large number of nonacademic staff, who manage the administrative shell and fulfill the essential requirements of maintaining plant and equipment, fulfilling payroll, accounting, and other human-relations tasks, operating foundations and alumni offices, and managing a wide array of student services from recruitment to academic advising to counseling and student activities programs. These services all create the context for the research university's success in attracting and retaining students and faculty.

The American university depends on quality people to operate and fuel the quality engine that drives the enterprise. Even though the physical plant of the institution stands as the symbol of its permanence and stability, it is the continuing personnel who actually define the university's success. Rich universities can purchase quality people for all their functions, including quality students, more easily than less well-funded counterparts, but institutions can never assume that the best people will always come.

Because the university is designed to be a stable enterprise, changing only slightly on the margin each year, it can sometimes be fooled into a false sense of security, believing that the quality people here today will be here tomorrow. Most of them will be, for the turnover rate at all levels of employment at most universities, especially research universities, is low by any standard.

Students turn over the most, with perhaps a quarter graduating, dropping out, or transferring out or in every year. Student quality is easier to change over time than other groups of the university's people because an effective recruitment and retention program can shift the student population's characteristics substantially within a two- to three-year period.

Staff, both those working in professional areas related to accounting, finance, and human resources and those serving in service areas such as physical plant, grounds, and food services, tend to stay in the university for long periods. Many public and some private institutions have excellent retirement packages requiring significant longevity to vest. Changes in the composition of this group of the university's people come slowly, linked to a significant degree to the retirement cycle.

Faculty also tend to be longstanding university citizens. While some mobility occurs in the early years of a career as faculty either fail to earn tenure or are lured away to another institution, by the time of tenure and especially by the time of promotion to full professor, the faculty, with some significant exceptions, tend to stay in place. Highly productive research faculty, however, are more mobile, and some number of these individuals will find alternative opportunities at other universities as their national and international reputations give them external value. The retention of these stars consumes some significant time on the part of department chairs, deans, provosts, and other university officers. Although the departure of a star is occasion for disappointment, it is often balanced by the acquisition of some other university's star.

Significant improvement or decline in faculty quality, given stable budgets, is the consequence of the retirement and replacement cycle more than of these high-profile departures or acquisitions of star faculty. This process (like the tenure process) demonstrates the university's continuing success. In much earlier times, the recruitment of new faculty was often an idiosyncratic affair with senior faculty, prominent administrators, and even university presidents seeking out the best and brightest through an informal network of colleagues at other institutions producing first-rate graduates with advanced degrees or identifying early to midlevel faculty who might be prepared to move. That system, often effective as a quality identifier, had some serious disadvantages. It tended to rely on old-boy networks of influence and relationship that frequently ignored high-quality women and minority candidates. Also, these networks tended to include much discussion of personal characteristics of candidates unrelated to their academic potential and accomplishments, such as race, class, religion, family, lifestyle, and similar concerns.

Today, the recruitment of faculty tends to be more orderly and reasonably public. Formalized requirements for posting job openings give clear guidelines about appropriate elements of a personnel decision. Although this system has improved the range of eligible candidates, it has some distance to go before achieving a neutral, nondiscriminatory field. Because the selection of replacements for retiring faculty is by far the most important personnel decision of the institution, any discriminatory influences that would limit the pool of high-quality candidates also constrain the institution's opportunity to identify the best candidates in the field.

University faculty constitute a self-perpetuating community. They choose their colleagues and their successors. The continuing quality of the university depends on the faculty identifying and recruiting nationally competitive colleagues, often colleagues a generation younger who should generally be better than the faculty already in the department. The best research universities have faculty who understand this renewal process and unflinchingly seek out the best to replace retiring colleagues, even knowing that the new people may well outshine many of the current faculty. Deans and provosts can monitor this process, and they can question selections that appear to fall short of the quality expectations of the institution, but the department (the guild) must in the end recruit the candidates. If the candidates are first rate, they will have other opportunities, and the competition for the best is intense because the number who can plausibly be seen as among the best is smaller than the number of new hires.

The challenge for the university is that this process of faculty replacement is often a small retail operation carried out over many years in different academic units: one chemist here, a historian there; one economist here, and a biologist there. Over the course of ten or fifteen years, systematically poor decisions will result in a much less competitive institution. Systematically good decisions will move the institution into the higher ranks of competition. Sustaining high-quality faculty replacements is among the most difficult challenges of any university. The pressures are many.

Institutions challenged by budget and perhaps enrollment issues may not automatically authorize a replacement for every retirement in every department. A department's quality, like the university's, depends in large part on the number of quality faculty it can acquire. If it cannot recruit a replacement for a retiree, it has no chance of maintaining or improving its academic standing. Recognizing this, a department awarded a faculty position may worry that if it does not fill the position this year, it may disappear in a budget crisis or reallocation by next year. This places great pressure on the department's faculty to hire someone, even if not first rate, for fear of losing the position if they wait to search for the best in the subsequent year. Deans try to avoid this problem by guaranteeing the position for several years, encouraging the department to continue searching for the best. But the fear of losing a position is so strong that many departments will settle for less.

As the department meeting begins, the department chair calls on Professor Gómez, coordinator of the search committee for the position in Latin American history, for his report. *Colleagues,* Professor Gómez says, *we've now collected information on the candidates, interviewed ten, and invited the three best to campus for visits. It's time to make a decision among these three. Your committee thinks all three are acceptable candidates with somewhat different strengths.* Associate Professor Sams asks, *This is not my field, but are these really the best? They seemed just OK to me.* Assistant Professor Chin says, *But if we don't hire one of them, I heard the dean will remove the position and give it to political science because that's the dean's field.* The department chair says reassuringly, *I talked to the dean, and he promised we can try again next year.* Professor Sanchez says, *Maybe so, but if we don't get one of these three and next year the pool of candidates isn't as good as this one, we'll be out of luck. Anyway, I heard that the dean is going to retire before next year, so his promise isn't worth much.* Professor Jacobs interjects, *I went to all three of the candidates' lectures and interviews, and I think at least two are pretty good—maybe not top drawer, but quite good. I move we make an offer to María García first and then, if she doesn't accept, to Pedro Salinas.* Professor Lucas seconds, and the motion passes.

Another technique for encouraging the departments to recruit and retain the best focuses on the tenure cycle. Most high-quality research universities will guarantee a replacement position if the department denies tenure to one of its tenure-track faculty. This is designed to remove the fear that a tenure denial will cause the department to lose a faculty position. Otherwise, the department might choose to apply a lower standard to a tenure case, believing that maintaining a marginal faculty member for life is preferable to losing a position.

## Micropolitics

Universities with their thousands of employees and often over a thousand faculty plus large numbers of students are constantly engaged in personnel issues of every imaginable kind. The big personnel crises end up in the newspaper, but any university's leaders from department chair through to even the trustees find themselves constantly resolving people issues. Being communities of long standing with virtually permanent residents, universities are endlessly political. Various groups negotiate, scheme, lobby, demonstrate, and otherwise engage in the competition for preference, recognition, influence, and compensation. The micropolitics of universities are always complex and multidimensional, but they follow different styles depending on institutional traditions, circumstances, and organization.

Institutions with strong unions tend to be much more overtly and directly political because these organizations have highly developed expertise in labor relations and can bring external resources and political pressures to bear on internal issues. Part of the union tradition is an adversarial relationship between management and labor, and university unions work constantly to increase the tension and hostility between whatever groups the union represents and whatever administrative officers make decisions. Even when the actual decisions about some matters may well rest with legislatures or other external authorities, the conflict requirement encourages union leadership to focus on local authorities, if only to maintain optimal levels of hostility and tension that serve to differentiate management from labor. Universities are more complicated than industrial workplaces, and while faculty may well be enthusiastic union members demonstrating for higher salaries, they are also guild members responsible for the academic quality of colleagues, academic freedom, research opportunities, and the academic authority of the faculty in matters of instruction and standards.

Micropolitics influences all levels of institutional management. Processes for the identification and selection of department chairs, deans, vice presidents, and of course presidents are all highly political in nature, even if they primarily focus on issues of competence, experience, suitability, and effectiveness. Search committees for administrative appointments are balanced politically to ensure that all factions have a voice, and lobbying around these searches (as well as endless gossip about who is thinking what about whom) is constant and often intense.

This highly politicized style exists as a subtheme of university life, but it is not the primary driver of institutional behavior. While university leaders spend a substantial amount of time and energy managing the political subtext of university life, most regard this activity as a necessary management chore, not a principal academic activity. The more politics the university must manage, however, the less energy and focus is left to drive the competitive behaviors that produce success.

Students, too, come to the university with important political perspectives—liberal, conservative, radical, or indifferent.

Some find student government a satisfying outlet for their political talents, running sophisticated campaigns for student government offices and then operating the often large budgets dedicated to student activities. Sororities and fraternities on many campuses play a large role in student and university life, mostly positive but from time to time a location for bad behavior with consequences that may well produce legal and administrative crises.

Students often bring their external political commitments inside the university as well, whether for support of causes related to the environment, social and economic equity, or international affairs. They organize, demonstrate, and advocate. Being smart, well educated, and effective, they can mobilize groups that either pressure the university to take some action relevant to their concerns or use the university as a platform to project their concerns onto a larger stage. Adept at manipulating the media and sympathetic faculty, students frequently seek to make the university a partner in the concerns that engage them. Since the student voice is multiple and diverse, this produces much controversy and activity. Most institutions, while encouraging student engagement, have developed effective techniques to deal with the now familiar styles of student activism. Even so, sometimes the behavior spins out of control and requires more direct action.

In dealing with the nonacademic activities of students, and often faculty and staff, universities require clear and explicit policies and procedures that protect the rights of all to be heard and speak but also preserve the integrity and safety of the campus. The purpose of activism is to move the university in one direction or another in support of this or that cause, and often the action requested by one group is opposed by another.

Universities are not authorized to serve as agents of social and political change other than through the education and research that is their function. Clear and explicit policies ensure that everyone understands the range and limits that apply to all, and the university must do what its policies and procedures imply. Some forms of student, faculty, or staff engagement have as their purpose high levels of conflict. The university operates best when it deals with these in a routine and predictable fashion, however loud or creative the rhetoric and demonstration. Routine and impartial responses to behavior, regardless of the political content, are the institution's best approach to managing the lively activism that occurs from time to time. The majority of students, faculty, and staff do not participate in these activities, of course, but they want to see their institution operate fairly, effectively, and impartially when confronted with such issues.

## Leadership

Leadership in universities is a complex concept. Although everyone thinks they understand what leadership means, in practice the operation of leadership varies widely. Each part of the university's structure within the academic core and the administrative shell has a range of leaders required to organize, direct, persuade, and drive institutional life. Because universities are stable and continuing organizations slow to change, their leadership is always in a state of gradual modification.

Department chairs, deans, provosts, and other academic leaders come and go on overlapping cycles; some come from the faculty and return to the faculty, although this is a more common practice for chairs than for other administrative officers. Deans frequently come from the ranks of chairs and often have shifted to an administrative track that will lead them to other deanships, vice provost positions, provost assignments, and eventually perhaps presidential or chancellor positions.

Universities usually do not have orderly succession plans, and the departure of a chair or a dean prompts a search for a replacement as if the departure were a total surprise. Of course, everyone knows that the term of these leaders is relatively short, less than ten years and closer to five, but nonetheless, the development of successor talent is a poorly defined process. The micropolitics of many universities sees the turnover of a leader as an opportunity to reset the institutional agenda in some way. Sometimes the goal is to benefit a faction that felt marginalized by prior leadership. Possibly the goal is to circulate the leadership in some orderly fashion, to give various subgroups of the institution a chance at driving the agenda. On occasion, the turnover is an opportunity to identify outside talent from another, usually perceived as better, institution to bring a change in focus or emphasis to the unit.

> *I hear Dean Wong is stepping down. Who will be the next dean?* Joe, the history department chair, asks his friend Susan, the political science department chair. Susan answers, *Well, it could be anyone, of course, but since Dean Wong is from chemistry and his predecessor was from comparative literature, I suppose the next dean will have to be from the social sciences.* Joe answers, *That's right; I forgot about that. Maybe I should nominate you?* Susan responds quickly, *Oh no! I probably wouldn't be selected, and anyway, no one who really wants to be dean will get picked. You know how our colleagues are.* Joe laughs. *Yes, you have to be reluctant, but I'm going to nominate you anyway.*

Leadership actually matters in universities, but it matters in different ways in different institutions. When a university is strong and performs at a high level of competitive success, the particular quality of any one university leader is usually not a critical question. If a dean turns out to be ineffective, high-quality institutions whose faculty and staff and students are first rate will continue to be first rate and will, within some reasonable time, help make a change in leadership. Especially in relation to the university's research agenda, the competition is conducted outside the institution against other major universities; internal micropolitics have less impact than imagined. However, if ineffective leadership becomes a norm, then over time the unit will eventually decline as its faculty, staff, and students respond to the poor management. High-performing institutions usually avoid this outcome, which is why they remain high performing.

University senior leadership at the level of president, vice presidents, provosts, and other institution-wide officers offers a somewhat different perspective. Even though the mythology of university management places great emphasis on presidential leadership, the practice often demonstrates wide variability in presidential significance. Midrange universities that have good but not stellar faculty, that possess good but not top-level research performance records, and that seek sustainable improvement to move into the top ranks require much different leadership than top-ranked American research universities. Good leadership is always better than poor leadership, but the cost of ineffective presidents is much lower in great universities than it is in the near great.

> *So tell me,* says a graduate student in the higher education leadership seminar, *what's the impact of presidential leadership?* The professor, trying to distill a complicated construct into a short response, answers, *If your university is number two in the research rankings and you hire a not very good president, at the end of five years, the university will still be number two. If your university is number 150 in the research rankings and you hire a not very good president, at the end of five years your university will be number 200. Oh,* says the student, *so a president makes a much bigger difference at an aspiring university than a top university.* The professor responds, *The president of an aspiring university brings distinction to the institution. A great university enhances the reputation of its president.*

The characteristics that make for effective presidents are highly dependent on institutional circumstances. The faculty prefer someone with academic background, a significant scholarly resume with teaching and research accomplishments at prestigious institutions, and some substantial academic administrative experience. Trustees tend to prefer people with business backgrounds or service in one of the science, medical, engineering, business, or professional fields. They look for financial experience, extensive administrative experience, and profiles that resemble their own backgrounds. Students want leaders who have empathy, a commitment to student governance, and a strong familiarity with student issues. They are often persuaded by easygoing charm and a charismatic style.

In practice, some successful university presidents have every combination of qualifications possible. If the university has an expert and experienced administrative staff of provosts and vice presidents, has a strong financial footing, and operates in an expanding environment with high-quality, effective faculty and good students, then a president can be relatively unconcerned with the operational issues of the institution and spend her time on fund raising, developing relationships with legislators, working the local business community, and in general preaching the gospel of institutional quality, improvement, and innovation to all audiences. She can focus on her role as an outside president, secure in the knowledge that the expert staff will keep the place running well and will find ways to cover any undeliverable promises made by the president in promoting the institution.

However, an institution may be in crisis, with an administrative support group of variable quality, a divided and often contentious faculty, an ad-hoc and fragile financial and budget situation, and declining student enrollment. This university may need an inside operator for president, someone conversant with operational issues, able to provide direction and authority for the changes and improvements required, and capable of engaging the internal constituencies on a basis of competence and experience.

If an outside president leads a university in crisis, the results will be poor. If an inside president attempts to second-guess and micromanage highly competent institutional leadership, the effectiveness of the institution will decline.

The quality and cohesiveness of the institutional governing board also influences the success of any university president. If the board focuses on the improvement of the institution, its members share a common expectation for institutional operations, and the president and the trustees share a common understanding about institutional goals, the leadership will likely be effective. However, in public universities especially, the larger political process can significantly undermine an initial consensus about institutional direction. Often a president hired by a board with a focused set of expectations can find that within the space of a year or two a change in governor and legislative leadership leads to a substantial change in trustee membership, cohesion, and expectations. One political agenda can turn quickly into another, and a president hired to fulfill the first group's objectives will have the wrong attributes to fulfill the new regime's expectations.

Other challenges that defeat university leadership are the constant crises that affect institutions, some self-inflicted and others external. Self-inflicted crises come from the mismanagement of high-profile athletics, the failure to observe appropriate procedures when making personnel changes or when handling student issues, or various forms of poor financial management. The resulting crises occupy the institution's staff and leadership, undermine the confidence of external audiences, and lead trustees and others to search for scapegoats among the current leadership. Sometimes they hit the right targets, but often they just sacrifice whoever is close to appease external constituencies. If the crisis does not lead to improved management, the scenario will repeat within five to ten years.

External crisis can also undermine the university's leadership. The most common crises are financial challenges brought on by national economic decline, state financial shortfalls for public universities, stock market declines for private universities, or changes in student preferences that reduce enrollment and its attendant revenue. Often universities address financial crises with stopgap measures and fail to make the fundamental readjustments needed to reset the university's budget to match its revenue. When the leadership is unclear about the nature of the financial problem, disguises the solutions, and avoids long-term decisions in favor of one-time fixes for structural financial problems, the effectiveness of leadership will erode rapidly. Open, visible, financial data accompanied by clear five-year budgets, as discussed in chapter 9, make necessary readjustments much easier to accomplish because they reduce the paranoia and suspicion that undermine the support needed to make significant changes.

Other crises come from natural disasters, earthquakes, floods, hurricanes, or tornadoes that threaten the physical integrity of the institution and place its people at risk. Responses to these kinds of events often test institutional leadership. They can leave the institution either stronger and more confident of its abilities to respond or weakened by a failure to engage these events with strength, openness, and effective action.

In the end, however, while the cult of leadership has many followers among those who observe university life, the leadership is never as important as the aggregate quality and expertise of the faculty, staff, students, trustees, alumni, and other institutional actors. An institutional commitment to performance measured against national standards creates a context for effective leadership at all levels. Absent that commitment, universities will find it difficult to improve and challenging to maintain their place among their counterparts.

The one constant in university life is the people. While we worry about the budget and finance, struggle to sustain buildings and maintain grounds, negotiate over curriculum and academic mission, and organize and reorganize governance, the university can never lose sight of the purpose of the enterprise. Universities, and especially research universities, are marvelous quality engines, operating to accumulate within their boundaries the largest number of the highest-quality faculty and students possible. By doing so, these institutions can compete with the best universities in the United States and the world.

# *Additional Reading*

A Sampler

An indication of the significance of colleges and universities in American life appears in the endless stream of publications analyzing, criticizing, describing, and engaging every imaginable aspect of higher education. This flood of writing appears in the popular press, in scholarly journals, and in books published for experts and the general public. Government agencies, legislatures, education associations, and special interest groups all publish reports, analyses, data, and other materials of interest. The items listed here serve as a somewhat eclectic sampling of the depth and breadth of this remarkable outpouring of commentary and analysis. Some of these items are classics in the field, while others have a more transitory value. Taken together, however, they provide a reasonable perspective on the scale, scope, and style of higher education research and writing. Those interested in staying abreast of the dynamic world of higher education should follow the two significant newspapers that cover the field on a daily basis. *The Chronicle of Higher Education* (a subscription publication available in print and online at chronicle.com) and *Inside Higher Ed* (available without charge online at www.insidehighered.com) offer news, commentary, analysis, and data on all aspects of American postsecondary education. Among their many useful functions they often identify new publications of significant interest.

----------

*2012 Giving USA: The Annual Report on Philanthropy for the Year 2011.* Chicago: Giving USA Foundation, 2012.

Adelman, Clifford. "War and Peace among the Words: Rhetoric, Style, and Propaganda in Response to National Reports." *Journal of Higher Education* 58, no. 4 (1987): 371–403.

American Association of University Professors. *1940 Statement of Principles on Academic Freedom and Tenure: With 1970 Interpretive Comments.* Washington, DC: American Association of University Professors, 2006.

Anderson, Eugene L. *The New Professoriate: Characteristics, Contributions, and Compensation.* Washington, DC: American Council on Education, 2002.

Astin, Alexander W. *What Matters in College? Four Critical Years Revisited.* San Francisco: Jossey-Bass, 1993.

Astin, Alexander W., and Anthony Lising Antonio. *Assessment for Excellence: The Philosophy and Practice of Assessment and Evaluation in Higher Education.* American Council on Education Series on Higher Education. 2nd ed. Lanham, MD: Rowman and Littlefield, 2012.

Baumol, William J., with contributions by Monte Malach, Ariel Pablos-Méndez, and Lilian Gomory Wu. *The Cost Disease: Why Computers Get Cheaper and Health Care Doesn't.* New Haven, CT: Yale University Press, 2012.

Bess, James L. *College and University Organization: Insights from the Behavioral Sciences.* New York: New York University Press, 1984.

Birnbaum, Robert. *Management Fads in Higher Education: Where They Come from, What They Do, Why They Fail.* San Francisco: Jossey-Bass, 2000.

Bloom, Allan David. *The Closing of the American Mind: How Higher Education Has Failed Democracy and Impoverished the Souls of Today's Students.* New York: Simon and Schuster, 1987.

Bok, Derek Curtis. *The Cost of Talent.* New York: Free Press, 1993.

Bowen, William G., and Derek Curtis Bok. *The Shape of the River: Long-Term Consequences of Considering Race in College and University Admissions.* Princeton, NJ: Princeton University Press, 1998.

Bowen, William G., and Neil L. Rudenstine. *In Pursuit of the PhD.* Princeton, NJ: Princeton University Press, 1992.

Boyer, Ernest L. *Scholarship Reconsidered: Priorities of the Professoriate.* Princeton, NJ: Carnegie Foundation for the Advancement of Teaching, 1990.

Bradburd, Ralph M., and Duncan P. Mann. "Wealth in Higher Education Institutions." *Journal of Higher Education* 64, no. 4 (1993): 472-493.

Capaldi, Elizabeth. "Intellectual Transformation and Budgetary Savings through Academic Reorganization." *Change* 41, no. 4 (2009): 18-27.

Capaldi, Elizabeth D., and Craig W. Abbey. "Performance and Costs in Higher Education: A Proposal for Better Data." *Change* 43, no. 2 (2011): 8-15.

Capaldi, Elizabeth D., John V. Lombardi, Craig W. Abbey, and Diane D. Craig. "In Pursuit of Number ONE." In *Top American Research Universities*. Tempe: The Center for Measuring University Performance, Arizona State University, 2010.

Capaldi, Elizabeth D., John V. Lombardi, and Victor Yellen. "Improving Graduation Rates: A Simple Method That Works." *Change* 38, no. 4 (2006): 44-50.

Carlson, Scott, and Goldie Blumenstyk. "For Whom Is College Being Reinvented? 'Disruptions' Have the Buzz but May Put Higher Education Out of Reach for Those Students Likely to Benefit the Most." *Chronicle of Higher Education*. December 17, 2012.

Carnevale, Anthony P., Tamara Jayasundera, and Ban Cheah. *The College Advantage: Weathering the Economic Storm*. Washington, DC: Georgetown University, 2012.

Clotfelter, Charles T., ed. *Context for Success: Measuring Colleges' Impact*. Washington, DC: HCM Strategists, 2012. www.hcmstrategists.com /contextforsuccess/papers.html.

Cohen, Arthur M., and Carrie B. Kisker. *The Shaping of American Higher Education: Emergence and Growth of the Contemporary System*. San Francisco: Jossey-Bass, 2010.

Cohen, Arthur M., and Florence B. Brawer. *The American Community College*. San Francisco: Jossey-Bass, 2003.

*College and University Rankings*. University of Illinois at Urbana-Champaign Library, 2012. Last modified 8/13/12, www.library.illinois .edu/sshel/specialcollections/rankings/index.html.

Committee on Research Universities. *Research Universities and the Future of America: Ten Breakthrough Actions Vital to Our Nation's Prosperity and Security*. National Research Council, Board on Higher Education and Workforce. Washington, DC: National Academies Press, 2012.

Craig, Diane D., and John V. Lombardi. "Moving Up: The Marketplace for Federal Research in America." In *Top American Research Universities*. Tempe: The Center for Measuring University Performance, Arizona State University, 2011.

Crowley, Joseph N. *In The Arena: The NCAA's First Century*. Digital Edition. Indianapolis, IN: NCAA, 2006. Last accessed December 2012, www.ncaapublications.com/productdownloads/AB06.pdf.

Cummings, Anthony M., Marcia L. Witte, William G. Bowen, Laura O. Lazarus, and Richard H. Ekman. *University Libraries and Scholarly Communication: A Study Prepared for the Andrew W. Mellon Foundation*. Washington, DC: Association of Research Libraries, 1992.

Cunningham, Brendan M., and Carlena K. Cochi-Ficano. "The Determinants of Donative Revenue Flows from Alumni of Higher Education: An Empirical Inquiry." *Journal of Human Resources* 37, no. 3 (2002): 540–569.

Desrochers, Donna M., and Rita J. Kirshstein. *College Spending in a Turbulent Decade: Findings from the Delta Cost Project. A Delta Data Update, 2000–2010*. Washington, DC: American Institutes for Research, 2012.

Dickeson, Robert C. *Prioritizing Academic Programs and Services: Reallocating Resources to Achieve Strategic Balance*. San Francisco: Jossey-Bass, 2010.

Duderstadt, James J. *Intercollegiate Athletics and the American University: A University President's Perspective*. Ann Arbor: University of Michigan Press, 2000.

Duderstadt, James J. *The View from the Helm: Leading the American University during an Era of Change*. Ann Arbor: University of Michigan Press, 2007.

Eide, Eric, Dominic J. Brewer, and Ronald G. Ehrenberg. "Does It Pay to Attend an Elite Private College? Evidence on the Effects of Undergraduate College Quality on Graduate School Attendance." *Economics of Education Review* 17, no. 4 (1998): 371–376.

Emens, Stephanie C. "The Methodology and Manipulation of the *U.S. News* Law School Rankings." *Journal of the Legal Profession* 34 (Fall 2009): 197–209.

Fairweather, James S. "Beyond the Rhetoric: Trends in the Relative Value of Teaching and Research in Faculty Salaries." *Journal of Higher Education* 76, no. 4 (2005): 401–422.

Fairweather, James S. "Myths and Realities of Academic Labor Markets." *Economics of Education Review* 14, no. 2 (1995): 179–192.

Feller, Irwin. "The Determinants of Research Competitiveness among Universities." In Albert H. Teich, ed. *Competitiveness in Academic Research*. Washington, DC: Committee on Science, Engineering, and Public Policy, American Association for the Advancement of Science, 1996, pp. 35-72.

Fitzpatrick, Maria D., and Damon Jones. *Higher Education, Merit-Based Scholarships and Post-Baccalaureate Migration*. Cambridge, MA: National Bureau of Economic Research, 2012.

Fogel, Daniel Mark, and Elizabeth Malson-Huddle. *Precipice or Crossroads? Where America's Great Public Universities Stand and Where They Are Going Midway through Their Second Century*. Albany: State University of New York Press, 2012.

*Global Research Benchmarking System*. Last updated 2011, www.research benchmarking.org.

Golden, Daniel. *The Price of Admission: How America's Ruling Class Buys Its Way into Elite Colleges—and Who Gets Left Outside the Gates*. New York: Crown Publishers, 2006.

Goldstein, Larry. *A Guide to College and University Budgeting: Foundations for Institutional Effectiveness*. 4th ed. Washington, DC: National Association of College and University Business Officers, 2012.

Greco, Albert N., and Robert M. Wharton. "The Market Demand for University Press Books, 2008-15." *Journal of Scholarly Publishing* (October 2010): 1-15.

*Guide to R&D Funding Data*. American Association for the Advancement of Science. Last updated 2009, www.aaas.org/spp/rd/guide.htm.

Halffman, Willem, and Loet Leydesdorff. "Is Inequality among Universities Increasing? Gini Coefficients and the Elusive Rise of Elite Universities." *Minerva* 48, no. 1 (2010): 55-72.

Hutchins, Robert Maynard. *The Higher Learning in America*. New Haven, CT: Yale University Press, 1936.

Jefferson, Thomas. *Report of the Commissioners for the University of Virginia*. A machine-readable transcription from the Electronic Text Center, University of Virginia Library, 1995. http://etext.lib.virginia.edu/toc /modeng/public/JefRock.html.

Karabel, Jerome. *The Chosen: The Hidden History of Admission and Exclusion at Harvard, Yale, and Princeton*. Boston, MA: Houghton Mifflin, 2005.

Kaufman, Roger A. *Mega Planning: Practical Tools for Organizational Success.* Thousand Oaks, CA: Sage Publications, 2000.

Kerr, Clark. *The Uses of the University.* Cambridge, MA: Harvard University Press, 2001.

Knapp, Laura G., Janice E. Kelly-Reid, and Scott A. Ginder. *Enrollment in Postsecondary Institutions, Fall 2011; Financial Statistics, Fiscal Year 2011; and Graduation Rates, Selected Cohorts, 2003-2008: First Look (Preliminary Data).* Washington, DC: National Center for Education Statistics, 2012.

Knapp, Laura G., Janice E. Kelly-Reid, and Scott A. Ginder. *Postsecondary Institutions and Price of Attendance in 2011-12, Degrees and Other Awards Conferred: 2010-11, and 12-Month Enrollment: 2010-11: First Look (Preliminary Data).* Washington, DC: National Center for Education Statistics, 2012.

Kuh, George D. "How Are We Doing? Tracking the Quality of the Undergraduate Experience, 1960s to the Present." *Review of Higher Education* 22, no. 2 (1999): 99-119.

Lane, Jason E. "The Spider Web of Oversight: An Analysis of External Oversight of Higher Education." *The Journal of Higher Education* 78, no. 6 (2007): 615-644.

Liu, Xiangmin, Scott Thomas, and Liang Zhang. "College Quality, Earnings, and Job Satisfaction: Evidence from Recent College Graduates." *Journal of Labor Research* 31, no. 2 (2010): 183-201.

Lombardi, John. *Perspectives on the Community College: Essays.* Edited by Arthur M. Cohen. Washington, DC: American Association of Community and Junior Colleges and the American Council on Education, 1992.

Lombardi, John V., Diane D. Craig, Elizabeth D. Capaldi, and Denise S. Gater. "University Organization, Governance, and Competitiveness." In *Top American Research Universities.* Gainesville: University of Florida, 2002.

Lombardi, John V., Diane D. Craig, Elizabeth D. Capaldi, Denise S. Gater, and Sarah L. Mendonça. "Quality Engines: The Competitive Context for Research Universities." In *Top American Research Universities.* Gainesville: University of Florida, 2001.

Lombardi, John V., Elizabeth D. Capaldi, and Craig W. Abbey. "Rankings, Competition, and the Evolving American University." In *Top American*

*Research Universities.* Tempe: The Center for Measuring University Performance, Arizona State University, 2007.

Lombardi, John V., Elizabeth D. Capaldi, Kristy R. Reeves, Diane D. Craig, Denise S. Gater, and Dominic Rivers. "The Sports Imperative in America's Research Universities." In *Top American Research Universities.* Gainesville: University of Florida, 2003.

Lowry, Charles B. "Year 2 of the 'Great Recession': Surviving the Present by Building the Future." *Journal of Library Administration* 51, no. 1 (2010): 37–53.

Massy, William F. "Academic Values in the Marketplace." *Higher Education Management and Policy* 21, no. 3 (2009): 1–16.

McPherson, Michael S., and Morton Owen Schapiro. "Expenditures and Revenues in American Higher Education." *The Williams Project on the Economics of Higher Education.* DP-27, September 1994.

Middaugh, Michael F. *Planning and Assessment in Higher Education: Demonstrating Institutional Effectiveness.* San Francisco: Jossey-Bass, 2010.

Monks, James. "The Returns to Individual and College Characteristics: Evidence from the National Longitudinal Survey of Youth." *Economics of Education Review* 19, vol. 3 (2000): 279–289.

National Academy of Sciences, National Academy of Engineering, and Institute of Medicine. *Rising above the Gathering Storm, Revisited: Rapidly Approaching Category 5.* Washington, DC: National Academies Press, 2010.

Pascarella, Ernest T., and Patrick T. Terenzini. *How College Affects Students: A Third Decade of Research.* San Francisco: Jossey-Bass, 2005.

*Portal: Libraries and the Academy.* Baltimore, MD: Johns Hopkins University Press, 2000.

Pullaro, Natalie. *NACUBO Tuition Discounting Study, 2011.* Washington, DC: National Association of College and University Business Officers, 2012.

*Redefining the Academic Library: Managing the Migration to Digital Information Services.* Washington, DC: The Advisory Board Company, 2011.

Renn, Kristen A., and Robert Dean Reason. *College Students in the United States: Characteristics, Experiences, and Outcomes.* San Francisco: Jossey-Bass, 2012.

Research Universities Futures Consortium. *The Current Health and Future Well-Being of the American Research University.* Amsterdam: Elsevier, 2012.

Richman, Barry M., and Richard N. Farmer. *Leadership, Goals, and Power in Higher Education.* San Francisco: Jossey-Bass, 1974.

Riesman, David, and Reuel Denney. "Football in America: A Study in Culture Diffusion." *American Quarterly* 3, no. 4 (1951): 309–325.

Rothblatt, Sheldon. "Global Branding and the Celebrity University." *Liberal Education* 94, no. 4 (2008): 26–33.

Rudolph, Frederick. *Curriculum: A History of the American Undergraduate Course of Study since 1636.* Carnegie Council on Policy Studies in Higher Education. San Francisco: Jossey-Bass, 1977.

Savage, Howard J., Harold Woodmansee Bentley, John T. McGovern, and Dean Franklin Smiley. *American College Athletics.* New York: Carnegie Foundation for the Advancement of Teaching, 1929.

Schuster, Jack H., and Martin J. Finkelstein. *The American Faculty: The Restructuring of Academic Work and Careers.* Baltimore, MD: Johns Hopkins University Press, 2006.

Scott, John C. "The Mission of the University: Medieval to Postmodern Transformations." *Journal of Higher Education* 77, no. 1 (2006): 1–39.

Shulman, James Lawrence, and William G. Bowen. *The Game of Life: College Sports and Educational Values.* Princeton, NJ: Princeton University Press, 2001.

Smith, Ronald A. *Pay for Play: A History of Big-Time College Athletic Reform.* Urbana: University of Illinois Press, 2011.

Smith, Ronald A. *Sports and Freedom: The Rise of Big-Time College Athletics.* New York: Oxford University Press, 1988.

Snyder, Thomas D., and Sally A. Dillow. *Digest of Education Statistics, 2010.* Washington, DC: National Center for Education Statistics, 2011.

Strauss, Jon C., and John R. Curry. *Responsibility Center Management: Lessons from 25 Years of Decentralized Management.* Washington, DC: National Association of College and University Business Officers, 2002.

Sullivan, Teresa A. *Improving Measurement of Productivity in Higher Education.* Washington, DC: National Academies Press, 2012.

Sykes, Charles J. *Profscam: Professors and the Demise of Higher Education.* Washington, DC: Regnery Gateway, 1988.

Tahey, Phil, Ron Salluzzo, Fred Prager, Lou Mezzina, and Chris Cowen. *Strategic Financial Analysis for Higher Education: Identifying, Measuring and Reporting Financial Risks.* 7th ed. San Francisco: Prager, KPMG, and Attain, 2010.

Thelin, John R. *A History of American Higher Education*. Baltimore, MD: Johns Hopkins University Press, 2004.

*Top American Research Universities Annual Report*. The Center for Measuring University Performance. Gainesville: University of Florida, 2000–2005; Tempe: Arizona State University, 2006–2011.

Trachtenberg, Stephen Joel, with Tansy Howard Blumer. *Big Man on Campus: A University President Speaks out on Higher Education*. New York: Simon and Schuster, 2008.

Veblen, Thorstein. *The Higher Learning in America: A Memorandum on the Conduct of Universities by Business Men* (1918). New York: Sagamore Press, 1957.

Veysey, Laurence R. *The Emergence of the American University*. Chicago, IL: University of Chicago Press, 1965.

Weerts, David J., and Justin M. Ronca. "Examining Differences in State Support for Higher Education: A Comparative Study of State Appropriations for Research I Universities." *Journal of Higher Education* 77, no. 6 (2006): 935–967.

Whalen, Edward L. *Responsibility Center Budgeting: An Approach to Decentralized Management for Institutions of Higher Education*. Bloomington: Indiana University Press, 1991.

Winston, Gordon C. "College Costs: Subsidies, Intuition, and Policy." *The Williams Project on the Economics of Higher Education*. DP-45, November 1997.

Winston, Gordon C. "Economic Stratification and Hierarchy among U.S. Colleges and Universities." *The Williams Project on the Economics of Higher Education*. DP-58, November 2000.

Winston, Gordon C. "The Positional Arms Race in Higher Education." *Williams Project on the Economics of Higher Education*. DP-54, April 2000.

Wong, Glenn M. *Essentials of Sports Law*. 4th ed. Santa Barbara, CA: Praeger, 2010.

Zemsky, Robert. *Making Reform Work: The Case for Transforming American Higher Education*. New Brunswick, NJ: Rutgers University Press, 2009.

Zimbalist, Andrew S. *Unpaid Professionals: Commercialism and Conflict in Big-Time College Sports*. Princeton, NJ: Princeton University Press, 1999.

# *Index*

academic advising, 105, 131, 132, 187
academic core, 2-12, 49, 63-64, 69,
    187, 190, 193, 195-96. *See also*
    faculty; guilds; performance;
    productivity; quality; quality
    engines; research; teaching
academic design. *See* curriculum
accounting, 29, 34, 70-74, 187, 188;
    all-funds, 74-77; budgets and, 97;
    improvement, 126-27; measure-
    ment, 108
accreditation, 47, 54, 97, 156-57
adjunct faculty, 29-30, 50
administrative shell, 2, 7-10, 70, 165,
    168, 187, 195. *See also* academic
    core; budgets; finance; manage-
    ment; managing improvement;
    measurement; quality engines;
    regulation: and governance
agricultural enterprises, 21, 37, 100,
    138-40
alumni, 18, 19, 41-42, 60, 63, 83,
    101, 102, 187, 200; donors, 96, 97,
    148; governing board members,
    159-60; intercollegiate sports,
    142-43, 145
American Association of State
    Colleges and Universities
    (AASCU), 37
American Association of Univer-
    sity Professors (AAUP), 66

American Council on Education
    (ACE), 38
American Indian land-grant
    colleges, 38
assets: faculty as capital, 61-63,
    64-65; from foundations, 75;
    not-for-profit net, 71; physical
    plant, 89; quality people, 187-89
Association of American Colleges
    and Universities, 36
Association of American
    Universities (AAU), 37-38
Association of Community
    Colleges, 36
Association of Public and Land
    Grant Universities (APLU), 38
Association of Research Libraries,
    153
associations: disciplinary, 97;
    faculty guild, 156; multiplicity
    of, 36-38, 66; national guild,
    121; professional, 123; regional
    accreditation, 156; student, 166
athletics. *See* intercollegiate
    athletics (sports)
authority: budget success, 87;
    faculty, 7, 28-30, 48, 84, 158-60,
    163, 193, 198; governance,
    158-63; governments, 84;
    students, 165-66; university's, 4,
    7, 167, 198

192; intercollegiate sports franchise system, 145; management of political subtext, 41, 52, 102, 178, 193. *See also* chairs and deans; presidents and chancellors; provosts and vice presidents

learning, and teaching, 46-54, 116, 121-25, 138, 176, 178, 183-85

liberal arts colleges, 22, 27, 36, 38, 45, 46, 50, 57, 99, 180, 183

major, the (undergraduate), 49, 50, 51, 69, 96, 108, 122, 130-35

management, 6, 13-23, 27-28. *See also* administrative shell; budgets; finance; managing improvement; measurement; people; quality engines; regulation: and governance; support services and special units

managing improvement, 63, 66-67, 118, 126-35; measurement, 96, 98-102, 105-10, 113-14; money and, 164-65; quality, 116-25, 155, 180, 189-92, 193, 201; recruitment and, 6, 189; regulation and governance, 156, 158-60, 163-71; support services, 136-38, 141, 150, 153. *See also* associations; community service; guilds; incentives and rewards; research; teaching; tenure

measurement, 18, 26, 96-114, 200; budgets and, 91, 92, 130, 138; citation counts, 43-44; data audiences, 101-7; faculty performance, for tenure, 64-66; improvement and rewards, 128-30; learning and teaching, 48-49; of quality, 115, 116-25, 126-30, 155, 157

micropolitics, 167, 171, 192-95, 196-97

microsystems, 129

missions, research university's, 1-2, 21-23, 33, 37, 38; of auxiliary enterprises, 136-38; measurement and, 107, 111, 124-25; of private institutions, 127; regulation and, 157

money. *See* budgets; costs; finance; fund raising; measurement; revenue

"money matters," 16-18, 69-70, 82, 164-65, 182

National Association of Independent Colleges and Universities, 36

National Center for Education Statistics (NCES), 34

parents, 18, 24, 31, 39, 47, 50, 54, 80, 85, 108, 134-35

patents, 10, 141, 149

peer review, 3, 5-6, 42, 57, 103, 181

people, high-quality, 7, 13-14, 18, 19, 20, 31, 60, 117, 187-201. *See also* leadership

performance, 6, 12, 16-19, 22, 43-44, 49, 53, 99-100; budgets, 83, 87, 92-94, 105, 109-10, 112-14, 115, 125, 126-30, 134, 141, 146; measurement, 103-5, 109-10, 112-14; quality, 116-21, 125, 181; tenure as investment in future, 64-66

"performance counts," 16, 17-18

physical plant, 18, 29, 62, 89, 124; outsource services, 137-38, 152-53, 185, 187, 188, 200

policy: boards, 126; governance, 168-70

post-tenure review, 67

presidents and chancellors, 15-16, 160-61, 164; academic management, 27-28; administrative shell, 7, 8, 15; budgets, 93-94; faculty governance, 164; faculty

presidents and chancellors
(*continued*)
recruitment, 189; finance, 74-75;
fund raising, 148-49; governing
boards, 159-61, 163; leadership,
195, 197-201; management, 16-17,
19-20, 27-28; managing
improvement, 128; measurement, 102; micropolitics, 193,
196; performance, 18; quality
engines, 13; rankings, 41-42;
reputation surveys, 41-42;
research, 59-60; technology,
52-53, 178; tenure, 65-66
private institutions, 12, 19, 20, 22,
33-38, 45, 50, 54, 67; content and
context, 184-85; finance, 75,
76-80, 182-83, 188, 200; fund
raising, 147; governance, 127,
158, 159-60, 162-63, 164, 170-71;
intercollegiate sports, 142, 143,
144; managing improvement,
127, 133; measurement, 97, 98,
100, 111; most rigorous, 65
productivity, 4, 5-6, 9, 20, 38, 43,
56; agricultural enterprises,
138-40; faculty, 61-68, 91-95,
189; managing improvement,
126-30, 134; measurement, 100,
104-5, 107-14, 116; and quality,
94-95, 104-5, 125, 126-30, 155, 157.
*See also* publications; research
promotion, faculty, 4, 63, 64-66,
163, 166, 189. *See also* tenure
provosts and vice presidents, 7, 8,
15-16; faculty retirement, 190;
leadership, 195, 197, 198;
managing improvement, 128;
measurement, 110, 120-21;
micropolitics, 193
publications, 5, 6, 18, 43, 151-53;
benchmarking, quality, 117-18,
121, 181; citation counts, ranking,

42-44; on-line access, 151; peer-
review, 3, 5-6, 42, 57, 103, 181
public interest, 9, 162-63
public media, press, 168-70, 171
public relations, 41-42, 52, 67, 102,
146

quality, 1-12, 18, 115-25, 181, 200;
measuring research, 117-21;
people, 7, 13-14, 18, 19, 20, 31, 60,
117, 187-201; productivity and,
104-5, 125, 126-30, 155, 157;
teaching, 121-23
quality engines, 1-12, 116, 155, 188,
201

ranking, 39-44, 58, 97, 102, 181, 197
regulation, 47, 155, 156-57; and
governance, 158-71
reputation-based surveys, 40-42, 44
research, 55-60; management,
13-14, 17, 17-20, 22; talent, 55-57;
teaching and, 45-46, 55-59,
72-73, 94, 107-11, 167. *See also*
academic core; performance;
productivity; quality
research universities, 1-12, 23,
20-22, 45; characteristics, 33-44;
top American, 1, 34, 42, 103, 112,
115, 118, 176, 181-82, 197, 201;
turnover rates (all levels),
188-92
revenue (income), 9-12, 17, 31, 114,
171, 175, 185, 200; budgets,
89-91, 94; contracts and grants
(state and federal), 34-36, 42,
58-59, 67-68, 76, 79, 102, 103, 113,
116, 155; declines, 163, 174, 179;
fees for service (health care,
medical), 59, 75-76, 79; finance,
74, 76-80; financial aid (federal
and state), 35, 76, 77, 79, 88, 134;
fund raising, 97, 111, 147-48, 159,